Time Travel through

Italy

Wandering with Fred and Dante

David Lundberg

Zante

Zante

Zante Publishing
P.O. Box 10794
Greensboro, NC 27404
info@zantepub.com

ISBN 9798618158060

Also by David Lundberg

Olympic Wandering
Time Travel through Greece

Wandering through Irish Legend, Lore and More
Time Travel through Ireland

Acknowledgments

I am indebted to the wonderful people of Italy and their beautiful country where I was most fortunate to live four fascinating years. This changed my life.

I will carry Italy with me forever. *Salute!*

To Bella Italia

Introduction

Our airliner crested the Alps, heading southeast into the morning sun. Jagged gray peaks with white tips rose beneath us, light mist curling around them. We descended, and after seven long years I felt I was coming home to the Mediterranean. Beside me were my seven-year-old son, my five-year-old daughter, and my wife, seven months pregnant with our third child. Our offspring were already displaying their future personalities. Paul was serious, studying the scenery out the side window. Erica was alert and vibrant near the end of a nine hour flight. Our other son kicked wildly inside his mother's belly.

The mountains dropped abruptly into the flat valley of the Po River. The river snaked through that green carpet, dotted with small villages with terra-cotta roofed buildings. All the towns sported a church bell tower like clusters of orange stones, each sprouting a single white stem.

Following in the footsteps of countless European invaders, pilgrims and tourists through the centuries, I was stepping in modern form down the staircase of the Alps into the ever-alluring peninsula of Italy. I descended onto a long, boot-shaped pier that jutted out into the Mediterranean, a land nearly surrounded by the sea yet large enough to form a major European power whose history, culture and accomplishments are studied and even revered.

Genetic analysis of the inhabitants of today's Italy reflect an almost perfectly balanced DNA profile of a people who are a mixture of fifty percent Northern European DNA (Celtic, Belgian, and Balkan) and fifty percent Mediterranean DNA (Spanish, Greek, and Levantine). This represents a continuous interaction of the people of Italy with regions all around them throughout history. This mingling was spurred by trade, invasions, conquests, and in no small part the beauty of the land and the people. The exact 50/50 DNA split suggests that neighbors from all directions were equally drawn to this seductive land. Italy has long been heart, soul and spiritual center of the western world.

The plane turned on final approach and glided onto a runway tucked beside the foot of one of the mountains. Our landing in Italy was smooth, gentle and welcoming. Over the next four years I learned that was a very appropriate introduction to this magical land.

We emerged from the airliner, everyone giving deference to my oddly shaped wife. My new boss, an air force colonel waiting in the morning sunshine introduced himself, looked at us and said, "I'm surprised they let her travel like that."

Ahead of me were the best four years of my life.

The Mediterranean Magnet

When I was a twenty-year-old college student, I worked for a month one summer at an American air force hospital in Spain. In my mid-twenties, I lived in Greece for three years. Now at the age of thirty-five, I had a four-year job assignment in northern Italy. I can't pinpoint the obvious attraction these lands had for me, but when James Boswell wrote, "All journeys end at the Mediterranean," I think he was on to something.

John, the young engineer I was replacing, drove us from the military airstrip into the Italian village that became our home. It was nestled at the foot of the Dolomites, the Italian pre-Alps, and a mountain soared above us, higher and wider than the other peaks that trailed off on either side. John chattered away, spraying us with volleys of disjointed information we couldn't possibly digest after a long, mostly sleepless flight from America.

We passed the town's main square. In the center stood a church with one of those soaring bell towers, a campanile. Ringing the square were an elementary school buzzing with cute children, a weathered government building with ornate columns, and a row of coffee shops with outdoor tables.

"The mountain is called Piancavallo, 'Smooth Horse.' It's about 2000 feet high, and there's a ski resort at the top," John said as his Fiat wound through the narrow streets of the village.

"How long is the drive up the mountain?"

"About thirty minutes."

I was starting to get a very good feeling about all this.

There were three small hotels in the town. Ours was named "The Oliva." The next morning as we ate breakfast, a postman putted up on his motor scooter. He walked into the small dining area that held the hotel bar, dug the morning mail from his soft leather briefcase and ordered a drink. The hotel owner poured him a clear liquid that flowed like vegetable oil, which the mailman immediately downed. The drink was grappa, and I later learned through personal experience that it was as dangerous as it looked. The mail carrier's crimson face darkened another notch then he departed, remounted his faithful steed and motored away.

I began to learn that life in Italy has a cadence. Everyone knows when to wake up, when to eat lunch, when businesses close in early afternoon, when they reopen and when dinner is served. The beat of life is very comfortable. When people know what to expect from generations of continuous culture, a pleasant peacefulness regulates their daily lives.

I grew up in the United States around Italian-Americans whose grandparents had emigrated mostly from southern Italy for economic reasons. Today, especially in northern Italy, I don't remember meeting anyone who wanted to leave. Life was good.

Italians, by and large, are very comfortable in their own skins. They are not intimidated by foreign ways. American sports, films and music are embraced. Even the English words that constantly infiltrate the Italian language are not bothersome.

Family ties are nearly inviolate. Adult married men often go to their mothers' homes for lunch. Having a weekend go by without seeing extended family members is rare. Telephone conversations between mothers and grown children are part of every day's routine.

The best Americans I ever met were those living in Italy with me. The land seemed to change us, at least temporarily, from individualistic strivers to social beings. We ate out frequently with co-workers. The constant arrivals and departures of military people on assignment were grand excuses to spend evenings eating, drinking and laughing.

After a restaurant meal, no bill was brought to the table. You simply walked to the cashier at the exit and related what you had eaten. The courses were tallied up and the bill paid. You never felt compelled to leave a tip.

It was the same at coffee bars, pastry shops and ice cream parlors. Many times my wife enjoyed a cappuccino and brioche with our young son, forgot to pay, departed the coffee shop, spent an hour shopping at the open air market, remembered the unpaid bill, then returned and settled up. There was never a problem.

Some of these habits were local, and since we lived in a village, it was different than a large city. But it is also true that while traveling south in Italy leads to poorer areas, the people become even friendlier and warmer.

Nearly everything was done in person at different offices throughout the village. Paying utility bills, taking care of car insurance premiums, delivering a check for the monthly rent. It wasn't just business; it was personal.

We rented a grand villa on the edge of town. It was oddly shaped with narrow balconies jutting out all around it. A terra-cotta tile roof crowned white stucco walls.

Inside the house our landlady had a thing about that terra-cotta color. An orange, overstuffed leather chair sat in our living room surrounded by burnt orange wallpaper. The kitchen's dishwasher had orange and chrome trim, and just when I thought I'd discovered every bit of citrus color in the house, springtime arrived and in the garden the roses bloomed a surprising shade.

Uniformity of culture does not mean people are alike; it means they share a common bond. Surrounding our villa were three very different men, but they were all very Italian.

Our kitchen shutters opened on a small vineyard that was home to an ancient vehicle that plowed up and down the rows. It was a 1939 Fiat tractor driven by a stout man with wide eyes glaring out above worn bib-overalls. Luti was on a disability pension, having fallen off the roof of his barn years before, then serving time in a rehab hospital. Within ten minutes of meeting him, he asked me to buy him Budweiser from the American store. Apparently his fall had made him a cautious man because for the next three years I often observed him, well lubricated with vino, leaving the local bar late at night, driving his motorbike so slowly I marveled that the vehicle stayed upright.

Beyond Luti's vineyard was a grand, redbrick villa where a tall, dark man sat on the veranda in the afternoon sunshine reading his newspaper. Abe was a retired sales engineer from a multinational chemical company, and he and I became good friends. We skied, drank wine and talked politics. Abe always did so with a comfortable masculine gentleness.

For the next four years, I constantly heard a phrase that described Abe and characterized this part of the world so well. *Molto gentile,* very gentle, very kind, very pleasant. It was said with respect and affection when speaking of someone who deserved the compliment.

Soon we were invited to dinner parties in Abe's home. We arrived early in the evening and moved through a series of entrees, wines and locations within the house. Life had a pace, life had a plan, and therefore it had a purpose.

Abe nominated me with considerable formality to his wine club in Rome. Soon I was receiving a small shipment of indigenous wines every six weeks. Some reds, some whites, always of good quality and reasonable price.

Other great wine producing regions of the world may have more consistent quality (California), more elegance (France), or better values (Chile), but it is impossible to match Italian variety. It is the land of the family vineyard, where each plot has its own label, name and character.

Although Abe spoke many languages fluently and traveled widely, I noticed he never spoke of Germany, never visited there, and never indicated he knew a word of that language. He and his wife traded cars every few years. French cars, Italian cars, never German.

One evening as Abe and his wife Angelina ate dinner in our home, we talked about life, good times and the eternal drama of Italian politics. I mentioned that my wife Vasso's mother was coming to visit us and that she came from the Greek island of Cephalonia.

Abe's radiant face darkened, he looked at the floor and said, "After all these years I hear the name of that place again."

"What is it, Abe?"

"In World War II, I was in the Italian army. It was a terrible time. We didn't know from one day to the next whose side we were on. Finally, our former allies, the Germans imprisoned us."

"I misbehaved so they sent me to the prison camp at Bergen-Belsen. My fellow soldiers were sent to Cephalonia where they were all executed."

He lapsed into silence, and stunned, I realized that this strong, gentle man had barely survived the war by being sent to the concentration camp where Anne Frank died. All his comrades perished. The fine and largely unappreciated film, "Corelli's Mandolin" documents the tragic story of those Italian soldiers. The book is even better than the film.

When we first arrived in Italy and were staying at the hotel in town, we immediately began looking for a house to rent. We sort of inherited the villa that became our four-year home from another American couple who rented it before us. As the young American woman showed us around, she chattered on about Italy, trying to educate us about the quirks of the house and about life in general in Italy.

In the middle of talking about our prospective villa, she stopped and interjected, "Children here are God!"

Strange way to phrase it, but as the years went by, I realized how magically correct she was. There are so many paintings of "Virgin Mother and Infant" scattered throughout Italy that if the artwork was not so varied and beautiful, you would suspect there must be a "Madonna and Child" assembly line hidden somewhere in the country.

In fact, the religious theme of these paintings is a veneer. The art reinforces again and again the priceless bond of mother and child. The adoration of that baby is a reflection of every Italian mother's love for her child. The beauty of the Virgin is an image of the desirability of Italian women. The great artist Raphael repeatedly used his shapely mistress as the model for his Madonnas. His early death at age thirty-seven was hastened by the intensity of their love life. He wasn't worn out by producing art; he was worn out by engaging in art.

During my years in Italy I was amazed at how culture shapes our lives. When I was growing up in western Pennsylvania, it was common for my young Italian-American friends to have many brothers and sisters. Those Italian immigrants to the United States were Catholic and prolific.

Twenty years later living in Italy, I didn't know a single Italian couple my age who had more than two children. All of our Italian neighbors imitated their friends, and the trend had moved toward smaller families.

We had great fun skiing with Abe and his family. Thirty-year-old Roberto was Abe's only child, Roberto's wife was an only child, and they had one child. It was as if all the love of children was funneled down into this one little boy. Devotion to family was still there, if anything, much more concentrated.

On the other side of our villa lived a husband and wife of a different sort. Anna was married to Jordano, a huge solid man with the heart of a child. He looked like a professional football linebacker. He often took our children on his tractor, happily plowing through the fields at sunset.

One Sunday morning I stopped at the local bar for some long forgotten reason. Jordano was there with his buddies. He offered me a glass of wine with the sincerity of a life-long friend. I was in an American hurry, and I regret my refusal to this day.

Some time later after living several years in Italy, I noticed a flurry of activity at Jordano's house, but I didn't pay much attention. A few days later I ran into an American friend in the Air Force officer's club. He walked up to me and said, "David, did you hear Jordano died?"

It was like a sledgehammer hit me in the chest. Jordano was the picture of health. No person dies at age fifty with rosy cheeks and a smile. Soon, small white funeral flyers were posted around town with his picture on them. The caption read, "The Gentle Giant." Jordano was gone; Italy went on.

Months passed and one summer evening I walked by Jordano's fields, golden with sunset. I looked toward the ragged, gray, pyramid-shaped mountain, rosy-edged clouds drifting by above it, and I realized I was living in a world that was born long ago and will never die. That sense of permanence makes you feel like time stands still. This is the closest we come in our lives to eternity.

The Four Pillars

There are four great pillars on which Italian history and culture rest. The first three are the main ancient groups that merged into what we now know as the Italian nation. Each pillar is distinct, and each contributed to what today is *Bella Italia*, beautiful Italy.

First were the Etruscans, the ancient settlers of north central Italy. Most accounts of this people describe them as a mysterious bunch who we know little about. In truth we understand quite a bit.

Next came the Romans, whose great culture forms the foundation on which much of today's western civilization stands. The reasons for their prominence are really very simple.

Third were the Greek colonists of southern Italy and Sicily. In the millennia before Christ there was considerable immigration of Greeks into the lower portion of the Italian peninsula. A talented group of philosophers, scientists, writers and profiteers. They built magnificent temples and were fine farmers and merchants. They constantly warred among themselves and not surprisingly, their descendants still do.

The last pillar of the Italian world is not an ethnic group. It is a foundation stone both ancient and modern, constantly evolving, reverenced and feared, trusted in a certain way and yet suspicious. The Catholic Church.

Over the centuries the first three clans grew together to form the people the world knows as Italians. However, the strong thread that provided a continuum through centuries of upheaval, invasion and foreign domination is undoubtedly the Catholic Church.

The Etruscans

The Etruscans dominated north central Italy from approximately 1000 to 500 B.C. They are often described as a puzzling people who left no discernible language or recorded history. Our knowledge of them comes from their burial mounds. Since they believed in a pleasant afterlife and built strong, elaborate tombs, we know a great deal about them. For a time they lived in harmony with their southern neighbors, the Romans, and for a while the Etruscans were more powerful. They were a strong, artistic and superstitious people who believed in divination (reading the future). The Etruscans gave their name to the region now known as Tuscany, and like the present occupants of that beautiful and romantic region, they were highly skilled artisans. The Etruscans were experts in iron, bronze, silver, copper, gold and pottery. Today we view their descendants as marvelous architects, sculptors and painters.

The Etruscan lifestyle was sensitive and bold. They painted in vivid deep reds, blues and yellows. Their cities were well fortified, positioned on some of the finest hilltop building sites in Italy. A network of excellent roads connected these settlements. Highly skilled in town planning and engineering, their irrigation and water systems were superb. But behind the massive walls, they built wooden temples, molded clay sculptures, and their dwellings were flimsy. They present the picture of a people who secured their existence and then "lived for the day." Unlike the Romans they were not interested in building empires for tomorrow.

Their tombs are embellished with striking murals of celebrations, dancing, hunting and war. The men of this society loved their women. A coffin belonging to one of the excavated tombs shows a striking model of husband and wife, reclining together at banquet, clearly enjoying their life (and hopefully, death) together. It is a unique picture of marital bliss in an otherwise brutal, male-dominated world. Murals on the walls of the tombs are painted in a realistic style with striking images of children milling around as their parents dined. Family life was crucially important to these folks. It still is.

Theirs was a loose association of independent city-states along religious lines, full of music and theatrical entertainment. Innovative and influential, the Etruscans loved life. Many historians say these people originally came from the Greek world to the east. Others say they formed by the merger of several northern Italian tribes. In either case like many cultures, their lifestyle seems more influenced by the climate, vegetation and topography of Tuscany than by genetic origin.

Because of this mysterious enduring influence, in a magical way we can travel through time, observing the ancient Etruscans in today's modern Tuscany. But that is a later story.

The Romans

For over one thousand years from 800 B.C. to around 500 A.D., the Roman civilization dominated the western world. Nothing before or since can compare. It began with Royal Rome, then it became the Roman Republic, and finally the Roman Empire. Whatever it was called at various periods of time, in terms of power and breadth it was the single greatest civilization in European history. Yet the reasons for its glory are simple.

The Romans were ambitious, magnificent organizers in the center of the known world. That was their genius and their great good fortune. The reason they conquered was first of all because they had the unique abilities to do so, but above all else, they wanted to.

Originally, Rome was a collection of Latin and Sabine villages, ruled by the Etruscans until the Roman tribe reversed that situation. They were unparalleled engineers, architects and builders. They were not a refined people, nor did they waste their time and energy formulating religions or producing masterpieces of original creative art. In those areas they simply "borrowed." They adopted the Greek gods, and they imported art forms. Like the Etruscans they were supremely realistic, and you can see this in their sculpture, which produced images that were often neither beautiful nor flattering. Big ears, flat noses, warts and bulging eyes stare out at the world. Whatever existed in real life was reproduced accurately. This was a culture with its feet firmly on the ground.

Organize, build, expand ... then build again. Great roads, magnificent structures, efficient aqueducts, and a highly disciplined army. What they lacked in imagination and creativity, they made up for with systematic thoroughness.

Great administrators, they knew how to cooperate, and they certainly knew how to pour cement and concrete.

The Romans slowly defeated and absorbed the Etruscans to the north. The Greek colonists of southern Italy and Sicily were never a real threat. The Greeks were also ambitious, but they were too argumentative to get along with one another or withstand Rome. The Romans eventually controlled all the Italian peninsula, Greece, Macedonia, Sicily, North Africa, Spain and Sardinia. Later they conquered Gaul (modern France), Belgium and Britain.

Today we look upon Rome as the bedrock of western civilization. Yet nearly everything the Romans passed on to us was borrowed from someone else. Their ancient religion was purely Greek. Their modern religion, Christianity, began as a renegade Jewish sect. Their philosophy was Greek, and their art had its roots with the Etruscans and others.

The Romans rose to great prominence on one of the beautiful, great peninsulas on this earth, one of the most desirable places on the planet to live or visit. Their descendants are delightful people, very comfortable with whom they are, and they are still great "borrowers." Foreign music, foreign words, foreign sports, none of the imports that other cultures view as "contaminants" bother the self-assured descendants of Rome whose ancestors absorbed the known world and yet remained "Roman."

As we travel through time we will see that in a way, their modern descendants still do the same thing.

The Greek Colonists
of Southern Italy and Sicily

For nearly two thousand years, Greek colonists and rulers dominated the culture of southern Italy and Sicily. They began to arrive in the 8th century B.C., spurred by famine and wars in Greece. For five hundred years, this part of Italy swelled with immigrant merchants, farmers and traders. The fertile coastal lands of southern Italy were virgin territory. The soil had been little farmed, and therefore agriculture thrived. The newcomers built magnificent temples, and *Magna Graecia* (Greater Greece) as it was called, also attracted prominent philosophers, scientists and writers.

The Greeks carried their intelligent, creative and argumentative spirit to this region. They also brought their highly individualistic political unit, the *polis* or city-state.

Syracuse was one of the first great colonies in Sicily, looking east toward the "mother country." Theocritus the poet, Plato the philosopher, and Archimedes the geometrician all spent time there. The great writer of tragedy, Aeschylus died in Gela where he was a frequent guest of the local ruler. The philosophical school of Pythagoras governed Crotone. Capua, Naples, Taranto, Rhegion, Ancona and numerous other colonies were ruled by different city-states back in Greece. It was a situation ripe for rivalry.

Magnificent temples rose in Sicily, and many still remain, often better-preserved examples of ancient Greek architecture than what now remains in Greece itself. Constant bickering and warfare between the various city-states weakened Greater Greece just as it did the home country, and by the 4th century B.C. the emphasis in artwork in Sicily and southern Italy shifted to sculpture. Building great temples was now too expensive for warring colonies that were financially exhausted. At the end of the 3rd century B.C. Rome conquered the region.

Sicily and southern Italy lie at the center of the Mediterranean Sea, and for millennia the Mediterranean was considered the focal point of the western world. The violent history of war and conquest bears testimony to that truth. The early Greek colonists merged with the local inhabitants to form a highly intelligent, warm-hearted, passionate and treacherous society. Contentious and individualistic to the core, they had no chance to stand before the disciplined and efficient Roman Empire or the series of well-organized conquerors who followed.

Later as the power of Rome shifted to the east, the rulers of the emerging Byzantine Empire reasserted their influence on Magna Graecia. Waves of immigrants again poured in from Greece and Asia Minor. Finally, as the Byzantines began to weaken a series of other foreigners exerted power.

First came the Saracens, North African Moslems who held the island of Sicily in the 9th and 10th centuries A.D. They were followed by Roger de Hauteville and his Norman relatives who united southern Italy and Sicily in the 11th century.

Frederick II followed the Normans, and his rule continued the rich intellectual tradition of the Greeks. Frederick's court in Palermo was filled with scientists, poets and artists.

After Frederick, Sicily passed to mainly Spanish rulers for the next five hundred years. Treachery and misrule reigned. Large estate owners enlisted defenders to protect their holdings from roving gangs of bandits. These protectors of the estates developed their own codes of honor and loyalty. In a region racked with dissension and mistrust, these loosely-knit bands of protectors merged into an indigenous organization that responded to centuries of injustice. These powerful men became known as the Mafia.

But the occupiers have now been absorbed. Today these lands form the southern third of the Italian nation and exert their own unique influence, formed through time.

The Catholic Church

At the death of Christ the Roman Empire ruled much of the western world, and it would continue to expand. "All roads led to Rome," and this was true for the two great apostles of Christianity, Peter and Paul. Both were martyred in the Eternal City. Peter was crucified upside down, allegedly because he said he was not worthy to die like his master. Paul was beheaded because he was a Roman citizen, and the tortured death of crucifixion was only used on foreigners.

Christianity was a much better "fit" for the Roman Empire than the polytheistic religion of the Greeks. The assurance of having one omnipotent God gave real confidence to a large group. The Greeks had fashioned their ancient gods in their own individual images. Brilliant, contentious, none of the Greek gods were all powerful, but they were interesting and highly entertaining.

The Hebrew concept of a single all-powerful God gave real authority, but theirs was an exclusive god who was just for the Jews (and their few converts), and that did not really suit the expanding Roman Empire, destined to encompass amazingly diverse people spread across Europe, North Africa and the Middle East. Christianity was made to order. The Roman Empire was ambitious, authoritarian and well disciplined. The religion of Peter, and especially of Paul, was single-minded, evangelical and certain. If it wasn't a marriage made in heaven, it certainly was a great match on earth.

It didn't look like such a wonderful arrangement in the beginning though. Christianity started in Rome as a small, persecuted religion of the underclass, mostly foreigners. Victims of persecution, fodder for gladiatorial exhibitions, blamed for society's ills, it was tough going. But the Christians gloried in their suffering, and it's difficult to defeat that kind of attitude.

By 200 A.D. the bishops of the church in Rome were no longer foreign immigrants, they were Latin, and the head bishop was recognized as the "pope." The religion had evolved from immigrant status to that of a citizen cult. Now things really got going.

The Church acquired wealth from the very beginning. Centered at the heart of the empire and location for the great apostolic martyrs, the Roman Christian Church rose to prominence. Persecutions came and went, but in 312 A.D. suddenly the world turned upside down.

A man named Constantine became emperor, but he wasn't a Roman. He came from the eastern part of the empire and although he was a pagan, his mother was Christian. Under Constantine, Christianity became the favored religion. Confiscated church property was returned, and large donations of land and money were made to the Church. Christianity gave the Roman Empire the spiritual backbone it needed to rule the western world. Throughout his life the emperor moved closer to Christianity, and he was baptized on his deathbed.

In 324 A.D. Constantine boldly moved the capital of the Empire from Rome to Byzantium, a small Greek village on the Bosporus in Asia Minor (today's Turkey). Under his influence and that of the men who ruled after him, the renamed town of Constantinople swelled into a majestic and influential city. The church was now split between its historic base in Rome and Constantine's new capital. In effect, the empire also began to separate, and these divisions would widen for the next 900 years. A painful rivalry and jockeying for power began between Greek East and Roman West.

History is written from a local perspective. And of course in the western world, we see history in our own terms.

Little appreciation goes to the Muslim world of the Middle East or to the rich, complex histories of Asia. Perhaps in the 21st century that may change. We shall see. Our western world has even overlooked the fascinating history of "eastern Christendom."

The Christian religion gave the eastern Roman Empire (the Byzantine Empire) the philosophy it needed to survive for another millennium. Unfortunately, the Western Roman Empire lacked the military strength to defend itself.

The emperor was in Constantinople; the pope was in Rome. Increasingly the Roman church took on a life of its own separate from, and often in competition with the kingdom that supported it. The Roman Empire in Italy came to an end in 476 A.D. when a Germanic general named Odoacer replaced the last emperor. What eventually became the Byzantine Empire in Constantinople came to an end a thousand years later in 1453 when the Ottoman Turks overran that city. Amazingly, the Roman "Catholic" Church survived both of them, and it still goes on today.

Through the centuries the western church's fortunes alternately blossomed and withered. A series of interesting men held the office of pope or "first bishop." Some were either great political leaders, strong spiritual leaders, or both. Others were corrupt, weak or ruthless. All were products for good or bad of the particular time they lived. The great majority have been Italian. As such, they often demonstrated the disciplined, stern, aggressive leadership of the ancient Romans.

The history of the Italian peninsula and the history of the Catholic Church are prime examples of the ability to survive through shifting allegiances. In the years after Constantine moved east, the Italian peninsula was harried by aggressors from the north, lured to this beautiful "Mediterranean Magnet."

First came the Lombards, an Austrian tribe, pushing down through the Alps. Then came various Germanic groups known as Goths. As the Byzantine emperor struggled to maintain power in southern Italy from faraway Constantinople, the peninsula was being carved up and the Roman church negotiated as best it could with the invaders. The Catholic Church was already a significant landowner, and in years to come the popes became outright political leaders and sovereigns.

By 700 A.D. these popes began to look to the Gauls, a French tribe, for help securing stability. Three remarkable warrior-kings: father, son and grandson gave the church strength during this time. Charles Martel, his son Pepin the Short, and finally the great Charlemagne joined with the church in what became known as the Holy Roman Empire. Pepin awarded lands for the church to rule, and eventually the pope crowned Charlemagne emperor.

These donated territories became known as the "Papal States." Geographically they cut right through the heart of the Italian peninsula, and they would remain the domain of the church in one form or another for the next one thousand years. The church had been a wealthy landholding organization with increasing political influence. Now church leaders began to rule their acquired "states." The popes had become princes, but they were dependent on real kings for security and defense.

To the north and to the south in the Italian peninsula, the culture of strong, independent city-states competed with the church's Papal kingdom. The legacy of the Etruscan north was independent cities. The heritage of southern Italy and Sicily was similar, the sovereign Greek *polis*. The result was an Italy of fiercely independent city-states surrounding the Papal territory in the center of a very divided country. This, above all else, is the legacy of this beautiful land.

Envious foreigners desired the Italian peninsula. The Moslem Saracens invaded Sicily and harassed Rome. Meanwhile the popes struggled in the arena of local politics. Since the church was prosperous and now governed provinces, wealthy Romans pursued lucrative positions within the church. Although the principle of priestly celibacy was preached, the reality was very different. Bishops often married or lived with concubines. Illegitimate children and other relatives became cardinals. Monasteries were profitable organizations, and wealthy individuals bought their way into control of these "cash cows."

Norman princes from northern France were lured toward the sunny south of Europe, and they replaced the Saracens as rulers in southern Italy. Like the Moslems, they competed for power with the church. Some reformed-minded popes struggled to improve conditions within the church, but Europe was a mass of warring groups, and the church was caught in the middle. The great question was what form the church could take and still survive, and in a brutal, evolving civilization that question was impossible to answer. The popes were men of spiritual authority who looked for permanent solutions in heaven and temporary ones on earth.

Then in the year 1095 an amazing event took place. The pope issued a call for Christians to free the Holy Land from Moslem control. The response was incredible. Violent, ambitious men suddenly had a focus for their energies that did not involve killing fellow Europeans. The Crusades were born.

Within four years the Crusaders took Jerusalem and massacred its Moslem occupants. The magnetic response to the Church's call to liberate Jerusalem was devastating proof of the pope's spiritual authority. Throughout Europe the motivational power of the Catholic Church was becoming formidable.

Meanwhile, the Byzantine Empire in the east was dying. Tragically, the Fourth Crusade in 1202 was diverted to Constantinople. When they arrived, the Crusaders turned on their Christian brothers and sacked the city. This was the final deathblow in poor relations between the eastern and western Christian worlds. Any sense of brotherhood between the Greek East and the Roman West shattered beyond repair. To the present day this wound has never completely healed.

The Holy Roman Empire was also struggling. Henry VI of Germany was the emperor and he married thirty-year-old Constance, daughter of the Norman king of Sicily, Roger II. It was a political move, seeking to merge through marriage the German emperor with Norman royalty who controlled southern Italy. They were married for ten years, and then a miracle happened.

The Miraculous Birth

Childless at forty years of age, Constance became pregnant. The pregnancy progressed in a healthy way until heavy with child and traveling south along the east coast of Italy to rejoin her husband Henry in Sicily, Constance felt birth pangs. The queen's unborn child decided to set his own agenda. He would continue to do so the rest of his life.

Constance ordered her caravan to halt at the town of Jesi, near Ancona. It was Christmas week 1194, cold and windy. The queen ordered a makeshift shelter erected in the central town square and informed her attendants that she would give birth publicly with the town's women free to witness the event. Surely her servants and the locals must have questioned whether pregnancy had unbalanced her thinking.

But Constance was hardly crazy; she was smart and tough. Without eyewitness accounts many would doubt the birth of an heir to a forty-year-old woman who until this time had been childless. Her supreme devotion to her soon-to-be-born son was obvious, and typically Italian.

Constance was correct. Crazy stories circulated that Frederick was the son of "a butcher from Jesi" or that he was illegitimate or that he was not really the son of Constance. In truth, Constance had lived in a convent until the age of thirty. Her brother William was in line to provide an heir for the throne of Sicily, but William produced no offspring, so basically Constance was "pressed into service." She was married off to Henry to preserve the royal line. It took ten years, but it worked.

Frederick was born the day after Christmas, December 26, 1194 in a town whose name hints of a messiah. Several days later Constance again summoned the town's women to observe her breastfeeding her son. His life certainly had an auspicious beginning.

He was designated the next emperor as an infant. By any account Frederick grew to be a most remarkable man and one of the greatest European rulers of all time. In her excellent biography of his life Georgina Masson states that among rulers in the centuries between Charlemagne and Napoleon (a period of one thousand years), Frederick had no equal.

But before "little Fred" could have a chance to fulfill his destiny, he first had to survive childhood, and that was no easy task. His father Henry had grand imperial designs, and since he was both German emperor and king of Sicily, the pope knew Henry would eventually place the church in Rome into a strong vice and begin to turn the screws.

However, medieval rulers had a habit of dying unexpectedly, and when Frederick was two years old Henry passed away after a brief illness.

This put Constance in charge of the Sicilian kingdom. She had much different ideas than her husband, and those thoughts centered on the survival of her son. Instead of competing with the pope, she enlisted him as an ally, giving up Frederick's claim on the empire. It was a smart, practical move, and young Frederick was proclaimed simply king of Sicily.

However, Constance took ill and died a year and a half after her husband. In her will she took the added precaution of formally naming the pope as Frederick's official guardian. The child was not yet four years old.

Frederick grew up in the palace in Palermo, under the care of designated protectors. How diligent they were and how far they would go to safeguard the child-king was questionable. How concerned the pope was in faraway Rome was also a matter of doubt.

At this point Frederick was a valuable pawn in an imperial power struggle. Ruthless men were waiting. One of them was Markward, ruler of the district of Ancona. He realized that the person in possession of the child held power in the southern kingdom. Markward schemed and bided his time. In the fall of 1201 he made his move.

He attacked Palermo and the city surrendered. Markward made his way to the palace and found the boy and a caregiver hiding in the basement. When Markward grabbed Frederick, the child leaped upon him in anger. The boy saw this was useless, cast aside his robes, tore his clothing and scratched his flesh, screaming loudly, "You shall not lay hands on the Lord's anointed." He was six years old.

Markward died one year later. The boy-king survived and continued to live in the palace with various tutors. For those who enjoy tracing bloodlines, Frederick was Italian, German, French and Scandinavian, but he grew up in an unusual way for royalty, actually a very unusual way for anyone.

*****

The young boy with the long golden hair walked across the cobblestoned courtyard of the palace. He moved with a pace and dignity that should have looked a bit silly for a child not yet twelve years old, but somehow it didn't. He walked more slowly than excited children of his size, yet more quickly than a normal stride of two children strolling, and the pace was very even. His small head was erect and he looked straight ahead. The morning sun was just creeping over the walls of the courtyard, it settled on his head, and the curled hair cast a slight reddish hue.

The huge double gate at the northern end of the courtyard was tended by two guards, one on each side. Twenty yards from the entrance, the child looked directly at the guard to his right and said, "Open the gate."

The guard sprang to opening, nodding to his partner, and they began lifting the restraining beam, fixed horizontally at chest level on the inside.

"Do you have an escort, your Highness?"

"No."

"It is early, Master."

The boy shot a glance into the guard's eyes and held them for a moment.

The guard bowed his head quickly and swung open the gate.

Frederick walked into the brilliant sunshine of a spring Palermo morning. He resumed his pace and walked straight down the street before him, heading directly north toward the sea.

The capital of the Kingdom of Sicily was coming alive in the morning air. Merchants talking, children scrambling about, the smells of horses, foods, and the sea mingled in Frederick's path. Palermo's odors and sounds and sights were like no other city on earth. In the year of our Lord 1206, this city contained the most multicultural society in the Mediterranean world. Byzantine Greeks, Moslems, Latins, Jews, and Frederick's mother's people, the ruling Norman-French, all went about their business and their lives. The young prince's grandfather, the great King Roger II had welded together and cultivated the kingdom inherited from his father, Roger I, into one of the very richest in the world. At one time there was more wealth in Palermo alone than in all of England.

The city's mosques, cathedrals, parks and palaces reflected this grandeur. The 400 minarets that once formed much of the silhouette of Palermo were now diminishing. During the turbulent years after the death of Roger II, the tolerance he built and profited from was marred by clashes between the Moslems and others, often fostered by the "others."

Roger I was simply an extremely gifted mercenary soldier and commander. He and his Norman relatives had been thugs for hire in southern Italy, and when they were enlisted to invade Sicily they were successful, and they liked what they conquered.

As their Viking ancestors, the Normans were successful not through their numbers, but through their raw abilities and ruthlessness. The two Rogers, one after another, centralized their power in the city and concentrated it in their self-proclaimed royalty. Kings by blood, … spilt blood.

And they were brilliant, decisive and powerful enough to hold it. But the old adage about a chain and its weakest link was certainly true for Norman Sicily. After the death of Roger II, the next two rulers were weaker links. William was a brave leader but couldn't measure up to the Rogers in other ways. Tancred was an illegitimate heir, probably more capable and certainly more popular that William, but he was challenged constantly and his reign lasted but five years.

This paved the way for Henry VI, Frederick's father, but Henry wasn't Norman, he was German. William had died childless, but before his death he married off his sister Constance to Henry who was in line to be the next Holy Roman Emperor. The main reason? William owed Henry money.

Henry was only twenty years old, and his ascension to Emperor was by no means sure, but he made it. This scared the popes from their elaborate headpieces to the soles of their silk lined slippers.

At the time of her marriage Constance was thirty years old, recently released from a convent, and she watched as Henry decimated her father's kingdom. Henry imprisoned, tortured or killed most of her relatives, then looted the kingdom, hauled much of the wealth to Germany, and installed his own men to manage the Sicilian kingdom. Not a marriage you would hope for.

But the blood of the Rogers ran through Constance's veins, and it ran icy cold. She put on a peaceful mask and bided her time. And her time came, unfortunately too short.

The little blond boy with the regal air neared the old Moslem quarter of the city, *Al Khalesa,* the Kalsa. Years before Frederick's birth, the Kalsa had been a vibrant, prosperous area, teeming with Saracen Moslems. Now the district was more quiet, and non-Moslems had slowly been moving in as the original occupants left the city for the countryside. Some had fled to North Africa because of the tensions.

Frederick continued past the Kalsa toward the water. As he passed people on the street, many recognized his royal garments and blond head. Men bowed their heads respectfully if facing him. A few even greeted him, always with a title like "Your highness" or "Excellency."

Some young girls turned quickly from his gaze and Frederick detected pretty smiles and flashing eyes as faces were covered. For some time now he had become aware that young girls and even young women were beginning to make him curious, make him wonder, and the wonderment was pleasant, even intriguing. His mind pondered this, as it did so many things. Up until now girls had been rather ornamental, if he thought of them at all.

He came to the sea. The harbor was to his left. He turned right. After a few minutes the buildings began to spread out and he turned down a broad street. To his left was a large well kept home with a stable beside and behind it. He entered the low gate and knocked on the wooden door of the home. The door opened and a well kept Moslem woman looked down at him and gasped.

"Your highness! My husband, ... my son said nothing about you coming. Please come in!"

Nervous, she quickly bowed. *"Salaam alakum."*

"Alakum ben salaam. They did not know, Madam."

Quickly she turned to one of her children. "Go! Hurry! Bring your father immediately! Tell him Prince Frederick is here." The child ran out the door.

She led Frederick to an adjoining room with cushioned seats on the floor. "Please, Excellency. Sit."

"I will stand."

"Are you hungry? Tea, perhaps?"

For the first time since he left the palace, Frederick smiled, and his eyes twinkled. "No thank you, Madam. I have eaten."

She returned his smile, and her anxious face softened.

"It is too long since you graced us with your presence, Your Highness."

"I have been busy with my studies, but perhaps now that the weather is becoming better."

Frederick heard the door open abruptly and a tall well-built, middle-aged Arab man entered. He wore dark riding clothes, high leather boots. A black-haired boy of Frederick's height followed.

The Arab went to one knee and bowed his head. The son mirrored the father's movements. "You honor us with your presence, Divine One."

Frederick raised his right hand beside his waist, palm upward.

The Arab rose quickly. "To what do we owe this honor, Your Highness?"

"I hear you received a new shipment of horses."

The older man smiled broadly. "Yes, would you like to see them?"

The boy nodded.

The Arab stepped aside and beckoned for Frederick to precede him.

The blond head turned to the lady. "Goodbye, Madam. It was pleasant to see you."

"As always, it was our honor."

Frederick walked out of the house ahead of his two hosts. As he walked toward the stables, the Arab drew alongside him and said, "Eight new horses, five stallions, three mares, all North African." They entered the horse barn, stalls on either side. "Sire, the new ones begin here on the right."

Frederick slowly looked at each horse, peering through the stalls as best he could. At the end of the line of stalls, the Arab threw open the back door of the stable, casting more light inside.

I like the last three, Abdul." Using his host's name for the first time. This was a signal for less formality.

"Your eye is good."

"Bring them outside the barn, one by one."

Abdul turned and opened the first stall, swiftly bridled the horse and led him out into the sunlight. He was a majestic white, beautiful head, flawless color. Abdul led him around in a small circle as Frederick and the other boy stood side by side watching.

"All right, the next one."

The Arab repeated the procedure with two more horses, a black and a gray.

Abdul stood with the gray. "Well, young master?"

"They all have the look of the breed." Turning to the other boy, Frederick said, "What do you think, Amad?"

"The white is beautiful, Excellency, but I like the black and the gray. Good spirit, good proportions."

Frederick glanced at the older man, signaling he was ready to talk.

"Son, put the white back in his stall."

"Yes, Father."

Frederick turned and walked slowly away from the stable and Abdul followed.

"How much for the black?"

"One hundred and fifty gold pieces."

"For a hundred and fifty I can buy any two horses in the city."

"Not a horse such as this, this one is so magnificent, the Prophet himself should ride him!"

"Seventy."

The man's eyes looked to the sky. "Allah, be merciful! If I give away a horse like that for such a price, my family will not eat for a month!"

Frederick smiled. "Your wife's cooking is so good you could afford not to eat for a month. Eighty."

"You bargain like an Arab, young one. A hundred and forty."

"Do not think I will be softened by Oriental flattery, my friend. Ninety."

"One twenty, and I will fast and pray for two weeks!"

The Arab boy returned from the stable and Frederick stopped pacing. "My final offer. I give you one hundred apiece, for the black and the gray."

"Done."

The Arab reached out and shook hands with the boy just as he would with an adult. "Those two will give you many years of service and pleasure."

"Only the black will, Abdul, the gray is a gift to your son."

The dark haired boy's eyes grew wide, and he began jumping up and down. His father looked straight into the blond face. "Young prince, my prayers are with you. You are as cunning as a Greek and as generous as the best Arab. And I believe you will grow as strong as a Norman."

For the first time Frederick laughed out loud. "Some people say I am all three."

He turned to the other boy. "Amad, let us go riding."

The Arab boy beamed and looked straight at his father.

"Of course, my son. Go get our prince's saddle and prepare the two horses. Have Ibn help you."

The young lad turned and raced into the stable, still half jumping as he ran.

The older man turned, put his hand on Frederick's shoulder, and for the first time spoke to him like a son. "I was not joking about Greeks, Arabs and Normans. To rule this kingdom, you will have to be all three."

"I know, Abdul. Your people are causing trouble in the south."

"They were badly treated by the people before you."

"But you remained here in the city. Do you still think about leaving?"

"Of course, but Palermo is my home, and when the trouble began, I had strong friends who were Normans and Greeks, so I felt safe enough. When you became our friend, it helped even more."

He turned and guided the boy toward the stable. "Let us see how Amad is taking care of his grand gift."

Amad and the stable boy, Ibn had prepared the black. A saddle that Frederick kept in the stable had been mounted. Its gold plated horn and fine carved leather turned the fine animal into a regal mount. The two boys had turned their attention to the gray.

The older man removed his hand from Frederick's shoulder. "I will have my wife prepare some food for you two." He turned and left the prince with the other boys.

Whispering gently, Frederick took the reins of the black horse and ran his free hand gently along the animal's side, occasionally patting him. Within a few minutes, Abdul returned with a small white sack.

"Here, Amad. Goat cheese, fruit, and some of your mother's fresh bread."

Turning to Frederick, he said, "Come young prince, let's get you up." He moved beside the horse, bent slightly, extending his arms and interlocking the fingers for the boy's foot. He hoisted him up.

Abdul then moved beside the gray, leaned toward his son and whispered, "Son, you have a sacred duty here. You take care of the prince. Don't be foolish, we hold his life in our hands. Be back in three hours. He will listen to you. No excuses."

"Yes, Father." With that the other boy was raised onto his horse. Abdul looked up at them and smiled broadly.

"These are the horses of men, not boys. They are broken, but not tested. You young men have fun, but be wise."

The blond prince nodded and smiled. He turned his horse, and the two of them rode out. Even at the age of eleven, Frederick was an expert horseman. He loved animals and the out of doors. Abdul's family was not the only one in town that sheltered him. At times when growing up, he was sometimes severely neglected, then pampered, then viewed as a pawn in power struggles, all in turn. It caused him to mature quickly. He listened well and weighed what he heard from all sources. In a city like Palermo with such rich diversity, he heard all sorts of opinions from all sorts of people, and he learned to balance and sort out the contradictions. He grew extremely strong-willed, but not arrogant.

After his birth his father had whisked him away from Constance and forced her into seclusion. The child was surrounded by his father's German colleagues. When Henry died suddenly, Constance immediately took possession of the child, brought him to Palermo and surrounded him with her Norman influences. When Constance died, his tutors and the streets of Palermo provided his education. His young mind developed like a fine set of scales, constantly balancing all the diverse stories he heard. He grew intellectually very tolerant. But the Catholic Church was in a very intolerant period. Huge struggles lay ahead.

In moments like this, with friends like Amad, he enjoyed his childhood and his freedom. They walked their horses uphill away from the sea and chattered and laughed like any other children.

It was an easy rise. The dwellings melted away and ahead of them were orange and olive groves.

"Amad, see that large tree ahead, above the others, on the right."

"Sure."

"I will race you."

Amad smiled and nodded.

Frederick looked ahead, tightened his grip. "Ready, … now!"

Both boys rapped the sides of their mounts with their heels, and the horses sprang ahead. The small riders flattened out, faces near the great necks. Frederick loosened his grip on the reins, moving up and down with the rhythm of the horse as it quickly gained speed, hooves thundering into a deafening drum roll.

Amad hung right beside him, arms pumping loosely back and forth, careful to give his horse full rein.

Neck and neck they closed on the tree. Thirty yards away, Frederick reached back with one hand, slapped his horse just behind the saddle, then lay flat against the great black mane. Fifteen yards, he slapped his heels against the black and yelled, "Go!" His horse surged ahead slightly, and they flew past the tree.

Both boys eased up on their mounts, tightening the reins slowly, moving more upright in their saddles. The horses slowly came to a trot. Frederick pumped his fist into the air, "I won!" And for a moment he was as unguarded as any eleven year old boy.

Amad's beautiful smile split his face. "You were lucky. I shall win next time!"

"Bah!"

The prince turned slightly in the saddle as the horses came to a walk. "You did not let me win?"

"Never!"

"Good!"

"Frederick, there is a spring just ahead. Are you hungry?"

"Sure."

Sitting under trees near the spring, they shared the food and looked at the great bay of Palermo stretching before them. After joking and teasing each other for a time, Frederick said, "Amad, you have wonderful parents. You are very lucky.

"Me? You are the prince of the kingdom."

"Yes," the blond boy said quietly. "I am. ... Come, let us return or your father will not let me ride with you next time."

Amad put his head back and laughed, "How can he refuse you?"

They helped each other onto their mounts, then started back toward the city. Amad looked at his companion. "This is a wonderful gift!"

They reached the stable. The doors were open and they rode in. Abdul was waiting. The Arab boy jumped down from his horse, but Frederick remained mounted.

"I am taking the horse back to the palace. Abdul, will you ride with me?"

"Certainly, young master." He turned his head. "Ibn! Saddle the dappled mare for me!"

"Well, young horsemen, how was the ride?"

Frederick replied, "Excellent. The quality of your horses never fails."

The Arab nodded. "Amad, how was yours?"

"Oh Father, it was magnificent! I felt like a prince myself riding a horse like that."

"You are a fortunate person to receive such a gift."

"I know, Father."

The stable boy approached with a lightly spotted mare. Abdul quickly swung into the saddle and said, "Go ahead your highness, lead out."

Frederick looked down. "I enjoyed the ride, Amad. *"Salaam."*

"Salaam."

The prince turned his horse and moved him out into the sunshine. The Arab man pulled alongside.

"Which way should we go, Abdul?"

"Any way you choose."

"Through the Kalsa?"

"Fine."

"Abdul, I walked around by the sea to your home, but I think it better to ride through the Moslem section with you."

The man narrowed his eyes and glanced at the boy. "I believe your mind is growing even faster than your body."

Frederick smiled and nodded. They moved their horses slowly down a narrow lane, walkers giving way quickly as they recognized the riders. Abdul had purposely chosen the smaller, more humble mount not to upstage the young boy.

"Abdul, what do you hear of the troubles in the south?"

Again the Arab was surprised. Frederick had never asked such a question before this.

"Nothing but rumors really. I have no direct contacts with those leaders." Then he added, "And you must understand that I would not like to discuss such things at length."

A few moments passed, and Abdul spoke again. "Know this, young one. If I ever hear of a real threat to you or your palace, I will come to you immediately."

His face blank, Frederick turned toward his escort and a small, happy smile crept across his lips.

They passed out of the Kalsa, reached the main street and turned up toward the palace.

"Abdul, in what are your people most skilled?"

The older man thought a few moments. "In general I would say they are fine farmers and excellent soldiers, particularly with the bow."

"Hmm." The boy nodded.

Fifty yards from the palace, the Arab halted his horse. Frederick turned with a questioning look on his face.

"Young one, I think it better if you rode in alone. Perhaps it is better if the guards and tutors did not know I accompanied you."

"They cannot tell me what to do."

"Of course not, but sometimes in life it is better if certain things are not known."

Frederick raised his hand. *"Salaam alakum,* my friend."

"Alakum ben Salaam."

The prince of the kingdom of Sicily turned and rode his horse toward the palace gates.

*****

The boy destined to become Frederick II, Holy Roman Emperor by the will of God, came of age in this environment. He roamed the streets of Palermo like an orphan. He grew up tough, hard and uncultured, but not uneducated. He devoured books, and his Italian blood ran hot. In addition to the horses, he became an expert with weapons. He loved animals and the outdoors and spent considerable time in the parks of Palermo. Along with his reddish blond hair he had piercing blue-green eyes. But in the end he was Sicilian, through and through.

At the age of fourteen Frederick was betrothed to Constance of Aragon, a marriage arranged by the pope. Constance was twenty-four years old, already the widow of another king, and the mother of a young son. She was elegant and beautiful, and she brought a sizable dowry including five hundred well-trained knights, a force that the young king desperately needed. However, Frederick's prize quickly evaporated. Within two months of their arrival in Sicily most of the knights and Constance's own brother died when a violent epidemic swept across the island.

Theirs was not a union of romance, but Frederick, always a quick learner, blossomed. From Constance he acquired the dignity and culture of a king. He already possessed the brilliance, boldness and craftiness of a Sicilian, and he was mature well beyond his years.

Plus he was lucky. By the time he was eighteen, hints of greatness sparked around Frederick. He was putting down rebellion and consolidating his power in Sicily. His main European opponent was King Otto of Germany, who consolidated his northern power and marched on Rome. The pope crowned Otto emperor on the condition he left Sicily alone. Otto ignored the pope and marched through southern Italy. As he was about to invade Frederick's island, the pope excommunicated Otto, and various German princes turned against him. He spun around and retreated to Germany to reestablish himself.

Frederick's advisors and wife warned him to sit tight. His hold on Sicily was shaky. He was very young.

Frederick ignored them. He gathered a few followers and set sail for Rome. Frederick secured the pope's blessing then snaked his way north through lands loyal to Otto.

While resting on a riverbank near Verona, he and his company were surprised by an enemy force. Half-clothed, he leaped on a horse, plunged into the river, guided his mount to the opposite side and escaped. He arrived in the Germany of his father as a stranger who knew almost nothing of the culture, climate and language. Short of money, ridiculed as the "Boy-King," he had no military experience and only 300 men. His opponent was a mature, battle-hardened commander. Over the next three years, in a series of brilliant diplomatic and military maneuvers, step-by-step Frederick outfoxed Otto and established himself as the legitimate ruler. He was daring; he was charming; he was generous to his supporters. He was everything that Otto was not. He was crowned and made a pledge to lead a Crusade to the Holy Land. The boy-king had become a man, and a legend was born.

He spent five more years in Germany, consolidating power, securing allies and setting up his eight-year-old son as the designated northern ruler. He schemed and manipulated the pope to set up his coronation as Holy Roman Emperor in Rome itself.

The great fear of the church was a revived Roman Empire uniting the north and the south of Italy and thereby squeezing the church powerless. The pope extracted concessions from Frederick that were meant to separate and diminish his strength and ambitions. But Frederick had his own plans. And they were grand ones.

He left Germany with great pageantry, led his caravan to Rome and was crowned by the pope in marvelous splendor. Frederick was like a Caesar, and he saw himself as just that. Within three days of the coronation, he set out toward the home he loved so much and had missed for eight years in the cold north.

During his absence, ambitious and powerful barons had seized additional lands and expanded their power and wealth. The moment Frederick crossed into his ancestral lands just north of Naples, he held his first court in the town of Capua. He laid out twenty well-prepared chapters of detailed laws governing his southern kingdom. These codes were precisely organized and efficient. They outlined how his kingdom would function administratively to yield power and wealth to the emperor. Then Frederick set about to enforce his laws.

It wasn't easy. Forcing strong landowners back under his dominion took discipline and power. In addition, the local Moslems now controlled western Sicily. Frederick moved with decisiveness and efficiency. The barons fell one by one. As he defeated tribes of Saracen Moslems, instead of slaughtering them, Frederick resettled over 20,000 in agricultural areas near

Foggia in southern Italy. It was a creative move to enlist his Moslem adversaries as allies. Undoubtedly, the king didn't want to waste fine talent. It was brilliant; his legend grew.

Frederick lived in a vicious world, and to survive and fulfill his destiny, he had to be just as brutal. Any number of examples could illustrate this. Here is one story.

Ibn Abbad was a powerful Moslem warlord in western Sicily. He was born in North Africa but came to Sicily as a young man, married a local chieftain's daughter and rose to become a strong leader. He began to mint his own coins and extend his influence. Frederick moved against him with a large military force. After a prolonged siege a meeting was negotiated between the Moslem leader and Frederick. A truce was agreed and Ibn Abbad was allowed to keep his personal treasure and given safe passage to North Africa. The Moslem leader's daughter struck a deal with Frederick that she would hold her father's base of operations intact to ensure his safety. Her caution was justified. On the voyage to Africa Ibn Abbad was thrown overboard and drowned. His treasure was returned to the emperor.

As time went by his daughter sent word to Frederick that she was weary of the continued conflict and agreed to allow the emperor's forces safe passage to her fortress high in the mountains. If Frederick's men could overpower the guards, she would surrender and their struggles would end.

The emperor sent 300 of his elite knights by darkness to her fortress, she gave them personal entry, but her men lay in ambush. They slaughtered every knight.

Frederick's main force arrived the next morning, and the heads of his warriors were all displayed on poles outside the Moslem stronghold.

Despite the emperor's best efforts he never captured or killed the Moslem princess. Ultimately she poisoned herself rather than be taken.

By 1222, Frederick was spawning illegitimate children with numerous mistresses, and Constance died prematurely. She was buried with great dignity in Palermo. Shortly thereafter, Frederick's closest advisor and the pope teamed up to persuade him to marry Yolande, the hereditary Queen of Jerusalem. The pope hoped to push the king on his long delayed Crusade.

Frederick was not excited about these marriage plans. Yolande was fourteen years old. Marriage among royalty was not about love, it was a matter of expanding power and wealth, but the only dowry Yolande brought was the title of monarch of Jerusalem, not much more than a name.

Frederick married Yolande in Brindisi upon her arrival from Palestine. The next few years before his departure on Crusade can only be described as tumultuous. The city-states of northern Italy resisted Frederick's attempts to consolidate them under his authority. The current pope was Honorius III, perhaps the most conciliatory pontiff Frederick dealt with in his lifetime. Honorius worked with the emperor to bring the northern Italian cities in line. Their joint aim was to launch the Crusade.

Unfortunately for Frederick, Honorius died in the spring of 1227, just as preparations for the Crusade were falling in place with a projected summer departure. The new pope, Gregory IX, was a very different sort of person. His first letter to the emperor was an ultimatum: depart on Crusade as scheduled, or face the consequences. Excommunication.

Though the new pope pushed Frederick to depart on Crusade he gave him little support in terms of money or warriors. The emperor assembled his army in Brindisi and prepared to set sail, but plague swept the encampment. Frederick and a close German ally were ill as they disembarked, and the German died at sea. Discouraged and sick the emperor returned to Italy, and again the Crusade was delayed.

The pope pounced. He excommunicated Frederick and resisted setting conditions for his restoration. Then Yolande died unexpectedly, and Frederick lost his position as King of Jerusalem. The title now passed to his infant son, Conrad. All had turned against Frederick, but he had faced these kinds of odds before. Incredibly, the bold Sicilian gambler re-gathered his army and departed. An excommunicated emperor, recovering from epidemic, sailing on Crusade to the Holy Land without Church support. No one had ever dared or even dreamed of such a thing. Had he finally pressed his famous luck too far?

Puglia

Southeastern Italy (Puglia), from which Frederick launched his crusade, is an area I visited frequently as an Air Force health inspector. In the late 1980s, the Americans maintained an air station far south, on the heel of the Italian boot. The base was large enough to justify my making visits every six months. It was located outside the village of San Vito dei Normanni (a saint of the Normans), near the sea 35 miles north of Brindisi.

The facility was basically a listening post. A huge circular antenna array dominated the small base. The antenna was over twenty meters high, built of aluminum rods, and resembled nothing so much as a vastly oversized circus enclosure for wild animal acts. The area inside the metal fence was the size of a small athletic field. The GIs dubbed the structure "the elephant cage," and the name stuck.

The air station was near the Adriatic coast, looking across the water at Yugoslavia and the other communist countries beyond. There was no question why the base was there and to whom we were listening.

Since my visits were fairly frequent, I became adept at flying there, doing my inspection and flying back home on a fairly tight schedule. But I always had to stay overnight, and my contact, a lieutenant named Keith, was a fine host.

The southern Italian towns were uniformly dark at night, and the buildings always seemed old and dilapidated from the outside. But as soon as we entered a restaurant, everything changed. Linen tablecloths, smartly dressed waiters and maitre d's, china and silverware. And of course, great food. One night as I watched my waiter expertly carve a wonderfully grilled fish on the serving cart beside our table, I realized how this region of southern Italy has developed over generations to deceive the taxman.

Unfinished homes, at least two sets of books for every business, ramshackle streets, so much is designed to fake out the revenue collectors. After centuries of oppressive taxation, anyone who doesn't use every bit of his wits to hold on to as much money as possible is not only a fool, he and his family may not survive.

On one visit Keith and I did a little touring. Just north of San Vito is Martina Franca, a *"trulli"* village. The trulli are small, white cone-shaped dwellings, unique to this region. The whitewashed walls of the houses are circular, typically with a gray conical, slate roof for a top. Their origin is mysterious. No one knows how or when they came into being, although it is fairly certain that hundreds of years ago, they were built without cement or concrete so they could be dismantled quickly if the king's tax assessor approached. What the royal revenue grabber saw was a heap of rubble. That old legend certainly fits the current culture of the region. This is time travel.

In the towns stretching north from Martina Franca, the trulli cover the rolling countryside like endless clusters of upside-down vanilla ice cream cones. When the best research leaves no real record of how these structures originated, the best idea is simply to lean back, open your eyes and use plain old common sense.

The trulli look distinctly North African. In a similar way, much of the architecture of southern Spain looks distinctly Moslem, a result of its Moorish occupation. So how and when did these trulli come into being?

In the year 1300 A.D. Charles II of Anjou, King of Sicily moved against the town of Lucera where eighty years before Frederick II had resettled the Saracens of Sicily.

Whatever his faults, Frederick was an ethnically and religiously tolerant emperor. His Moslem warriors and bodyguards were a valuable and essential part of his armies. They served him well. After Frederick resettled the Saracens in the deserted town of Lucera, they prospered and the population of the town quickly grew to over 50,000. It was a thriving agricultural community.

With the support of the pope, Charles II destroyed Moslem Lucera. All the inhabitants were either killed, forced to convert to Christianity or resettled elsewhere in southern Italy. The relocated Moslems were largely sold into slavery. Some were sent out of Italy. Others became servants within the country.

In her unique and well-researched book, "Muslims in Medieval Italy," Julie Taylor pieces together the fate of these "infidels." The records are better defined for Muslims who were relocated near Lucera or in Naples, and the picture isn't pretty. However, a good number were resettled as far away as the region from Bari to Otranto, the heel of the Italian peninsula. Many of these former Lucerans ended up as servants. Some escaped.

This is the region of today's trulli, a farming area that fit the skills of the Saracens well. To survive, the Moslems had to keep their identity as vague as possible. Likewise, the origin of the trulli remains mysterious. But as we look back over the centuries, perhaps it's not that great a puzzle.

Keith and I traveled around this magical looking region until nightfall. We drove into a large town. The city center rose like a fortress on a hill in a maze of narrow, winding cobblestone streets. Dark stone buildings formed walls on each side of us. We climbed the ascending lanes until Keith pointed to a dimly lit doorway draped with a curtain. Inside the restaurant was multi-leveled, creeping upward like the passageways outside. A dark young man silently gazed down from behind a black piano. He descended a few steps and ushered us to a low table lit by a single candle. We could just as easily have been in North Africa.

The meal was excellent. We were the only patrons. We sat beside a window; thick blackness hovered outside. Keith said,

"When I arrived at San Vito I lived in the village outside the air force station with my wife and son until a duplex on base came available. All the married folks must work their way up the waiting list for housing."

"About a week after we moved into our house in the village there was a knock at the door. One of the locals dropped by to introduce himself. He was a member of the local *'vigilantes.'* He told us we should pay him a fee every month, and he would guarantee our home was never burglarized."

"How much was the fee?" I asked.

"Fifteen dollars."

"Did you pay?"

"Of course. Everyone does. It's cheap insurance."

"So they don't use the word *'Mafia.'*"

"No. But it's the same thing."

"Ever have any break-ins?"

"No. They are absolutely reliable."

The next morning Keith dropped me off at the Brindisi airport to catch my 10 a.m. Alitalia flight back to Rome, then Venice. When I entered the terminal I noticed long lines and an unusual amount of talking and chatter. I went to the ticket counter, checked in and asked the girl what was going on.

"There's a strike of baggage handlers in Rome. Your flight is delayed."

"How long is the delay?"

"The strike is until noon. Your flight should take off sometime after that."

It did. I arrived in Venice two hours later than expected.

In Italy labor strikes are frequent and short. To foreigners these events seem strange. When I grew up in America strikes were generally serious affairs. Real contests between management and labor designed to exact concessions for workers. They took on the atmosphere of boxing matches or military skirmishes. The outcome and the ultimate winner, management or labor, were in doubt. Strikes could last for months and be really disruptive to service, profits and the paychecks of employees who waged war against their employer.

Not so in Italy. Strikes here seemed to be token protests. Of short duration, designed to get someone's attention.

I got the idea that as in so many other ways in this country, these strikes were mostly theatrical. Basically drama, in the end a good show. Life went on without a great deal of disruption. As always in Italy, living is what really matters.

On to the Crusade

Frederick's crusade to the Holy Land was a daring, heroic gamble. He sailed to Palestine from southern Italy as an excommunicated king with a small army and no papal support. The bold Crusader spirit of the past century was dead, and the Christian knights of Palestine couldn't decide if they should support him. Frederick negotiated with the Moslem ruler, gaining the cities of Jerusalem, Bethlehem and Nazareth for the Empire in addition to a corridor insuring safe passage of Christian pilgrims from the sea to Jerusalem. He did it without war and without concessions to the Arabs. It was stunning.

The pontiff was furious, and the legend of Frederick grew.

Meanwhile, back in Italy Pope Gregory directed his armies to attack Frederick's southern Italian kingdom. However, the pope's position was not that strong. After excommunicating Frederick, local citizens loyal to the emperor had actually driven Gregory from Rome. Frederick's supporters in Germany would not turn against the emperor. Though resistant to Frederick, the northern Italian cities would not actively support the pope in the attack. Frederick's allies in southern Italy put up a strong defense.

Even in Palestine the emperor was quite aware of what was happening. He returned to Sicily just one year after his departure. The pope had been spreading stories that Frederick was dead, and when he arrived alive and triumphant, his allies gained new energy. The emperor hurled his forces at the papal armies and pushed them back to Rome. However, here lay the fundamental problem that would plague Frederick for the rest of his life. He needed the "blessing" of the Church more than the pope needed him.

Frederick met Gregory near Rome and all "appeared" forgiven. The pope really had no choice. The ban of excommunication was lifted and the emperor reinstated as a good Catholic. Frederick returned to his southern kingdom and entered the best period of his life.

During the next few years, the brilliance of Frederick blazed like a diamond in a spotlight. He studied the laws of his diverse kingdom: the codes of the Italians, Normans, Byzantine Greeks and Moslems, then formulated an extensive code of law echoing the ancient precepts of the emperor Justinian. Frederick launched Europe out of medieval feudalism into the modern world. He saw himself as God's emperor, responsible for the lives of Europeans during their sojourn on this earth. He believed that his duty was the administration of justice for his subjects. As far as their spiritual welfare and eternal salvation, that was the domain of the church.

In Rome the popes were at the height of their power, and they understood all too clearly that this vision of Frederick would squash their temporal power. The emperor saw "Justice" as the god of the secular world, and he saw himself as God's appointed administrator. Here lies the real essence of the history of Italy and the evolution of Western Europe. The continuing tension and struggle between a powerful Catholic church and rising national leaders. Frederick gave birth to secular Europe, ... the Europe of today.

However, he was too intelligent, too early and he was up against a powerful church and strong, individualistic city-states. Frederick was a brilliant administrator, but his finances were limited.

Scholars, mathematicians, astrologers, scientists and poets flocked to his court. Frederick was a true Renaissance man, hundreds of years before the word was even imagined.

His legal code was known as the *Liber Augustalis*. In its construction Frederick's Norman ancestry is clear. Striking was the revolutionary concept that "all citizens are equal before the law." He severely limited the ability of the church, nobles and individual cities to own lands for their own income. His laws were harsh and inflexible, designed to centralize power in his government. He appointed a series of judges whose terms of service were strictly limited and continued only after strong review. The head magistrates could not be citizens of their regions or married to citizens. They were paid not with awards of property, but in salaries from the state.

Under his code the status of women was remarkable for the time. Rape and kidnapping became capital offenses, and women could own and inherit property just like men. Punishment of corrupt government magistrates was severe. Bribery was outlawed. A main result of the emperor's code was removing the common man from abuse by government officials. Another result was shifting revenue from the local barons to the emperor's personal treasury. He would need every ounce of wealth for his coming battles with the popes. In the end it would not be enough.

It is almost impossible to imagine the wealth of Sicily and the grandeur of Frederick's court. Sicily and southern Italy were fertile breadbaskets at the center of the western world and the main shipping routes. Although the emperor rigidly controlled the economy at the government level, inside his realm market forces were given a very free hand. Sort of like China today. His legislative rules were strict and harsh, and he extracted heavy taxes to run the empire. Because his administration was so efficient and his empire so rich, this worked for a while. To realize he governed and ran the Holy Roman Empire, conducted expensive wars without Church support (indeed, with the Church's active opposition), all from the revenues of Sicily and southern Italy is beyond comprehension today. The result was he impoverished one of the naturally richest areas of the world. That, combined with the subsequent brutal oppression and neglect of these lands is truly a tragedy of epic proportions.

Frederick spoke nine languages, and he could read and write in seven of them. He was basically a tolerant Christian who saw himself as the Lord's anointed. But he was on a collision course with a Church that had become a secular power. After he settled the Saracens on the Italian mainland Frederick enlisted them in his army and as personal bodyguards. He had an unquenchable thirst for knowledge, rewrote an Arab book on ornithology and was a keen student of astrology.

*****

In search of Frederick's book, I scan sales outlets on the Internet and find modern translations available and highly rated by current critics, but quite expensive. Rather than plunk down the money sight unseen, I drive to my local university library and search the computerized catalogue. Deep in the library's basement I walk along the dark stacks and discover the designated row. Halfway down the aisle, the number system points to the top shelf. I find a stool, reach up and find two massive copies printed in 1943, but in near perfect condition.

Frederick's book on falconry is a wonder. Eight hundred years old, it remains the definitive text on this fascinating sport and gives us hints of the emperor's complex character. He was both a lover of nature and a precise scientist. Hunting remains a passion with many individuals today, but in the days before accurate rifles and guns existed, falcons were bred, trained and employed for this pastime, their handlers engrossed in working with a living creature rather than inanimate firearms of wood and metal. Frederick's book begins with an argument of how falconry is the noblest form of hunting. He describes it as an "art."

"The Art of Falconry" covers nearly all aspects of the subject in addition to a fine, extensive overview of the life of birds in general. Types of birds, habitats, feeding and nesting patterns, migration routes, detailed anatomy, hunting methods, training, varieties of birds of prey, the book goes on and on. It is precise, concise and encyclopedic, filled with wonderful illustrations of falcons and their handlers. Frederick's writing is comprehensive and clear, the work of a highly rational and scientific mind that was completely absorbed with its passion for the sport.

I sit on the stool in the dark basement and leaf through the book, reading various sections. The modern bound volume is fifty years old, but I travel much further back in time. Frederick's words, ancient but alive and accurate, and the detailed sketches make this book one more time machine. His book remained "the" guide to falconry for centuries. Today the finest original copy resides in the Vatican Library.

The translators include sections on Frederick's scholarship including his study of Aristotle's writings on birds, in addition to studies by Pliny, research from the Middle East and northern Europe all the way to Iceland with its gyrfalcons. Modern photographs display fine images of the emperor's numerous hunting lodges and castles in southern Italy including the crown jewel, Castel del Monte.

Looking out on the vast, semi-barren plains of Puglia Frederick felt the extent of his realm. The great skies stretching to the horizon were a universe for his birds of prey to practice their skills. Puglia had the added advantage of placing

Frederick and his armies much closer to Rome and his northern opponents. His loyal Moslem bodyguards and soldiers were headquartered nearby in Lucera, as was the permanent residence of his harem. Better in many ways to be here than in remote Sicily.

For me the book's most striking picture is the Cathedral at Bitonto along with a description of Frederick's funeral procession, the body of the emperor followed by six companies of weeping Moslem Saracens marching past the Christian church.

*****

Frederick founded the University of Naples, the first and only literary association in southern Italy for hundreds of years. He gave birth to secular education rather than religious-oriented learning, and this put his university in direct competition with church-dominated schools in places like Bologna. He was a Christian emperor, a mathematician and a poet who maintained an Oriental harem of Moslem dancing girls and kept his successive wives in seclusion. His court was the first to use a common Italian language (Sicilian), rather than Latin, as a literary form. Dante followed in his footsteps.

Frederick forbid physicians to act as pharmacists in order to squash the inflated price of medicines. He outlawed trials by ordeal or duels as unjust.

In addition to the emperor's passion for falconry he maintained a mobile zoo of exotic animals that traveled around Europe with him as he waged war with the popes and their allies. He posed difficult problems for Leonardo Fibonacci of Pisa, the greatest mathematician of the day. Stubborn, brilliant and temperamental, Frederick was a prime example of the unique heritage of Sicily. He became known as *stupor mundi*, the wonder of the world.

In addition to the intellectual flowering of his court, the farmlands of his kingdom bloomed. Agriculture and trade were extremely prosperous. Taxation was heavy, and the farms were state controlled. But Sicily and southern Italy were so rich in products and commerce that Frederick was able to finance his expensive military campaigns.

Sicily

One day as I sat at my desk in the American air force clinic in northern Italy, my phone rang. I picked it up.

"Major Lundberg."

"David, this is Colonel McGhee." The headquarters engineer in Germany. "I have a new engineer down in Sicily. He's young and needs a little help. Would you go down there and give him some guidance?"

"What do you have in mind, sir?"

"Oh, a three day staff assistance visit should do it. You could go down, check it out, then depending on what you find there, perhaps every six months until he gets his feet on the ground."

"Colonel, I don't mind. I'm doing staff assistance visits all over Italy. One more doesn't make a difference."

"Fine. I'll talk to your commander. We'll pay for it."

"When do you want me to go?"

"As soon as you can."

"O.K., sir. I'll call down there and make the arrangements."

"Good. Thanks, David." He hung up.

Three weeks later I was on an Alitalia flight to Sicily. I loved doing this. Typically, I flew from Venice to Rome, changed planes, then went on to my final destination.

Ninety percent of the passengers on these flights were middle-aged businessmen dressed in gray suits, carrying briefcases. Protruding through coat buttons, a round belly proclaimed each fellow's prosperity. The pilots of the airliners were all men. The flight attendants were all female, young and attractive with warm smiles, plunging necklines and tight skirts. In America we would call this sexist. Over here we called it Italian.

My plane from Rome headed south. We left the mainland, crossed a short stretch of water and Sicily was suddenly beneath us. Within a few minutes Mount Etna passed below, barren gray peak steaming, patiently preparing for its next eruption.

I landed in Catania. The odor of chain smokers filled the terminal, and the floor was a carpet of carelessly discarded cigarette butts. I walked to the rental car cubicle and looked down at a young brunette with enormous, perfect eyes. For a second I felt I was falling into those bottomless wells of beauty.

"Belli ochi," I said. Beautiful eyes.

"Grazie." Her smile was instant, natural, and intoxicating. It is no wonder that Italian women are so captivating to foreigners. They are so comfortable and un-self conscious about displaying their attractiveness.

Soon I was zooming over the hills south of Catania in my rented Alfa Romeo, the quintessential Italian car. Powerful, light, built for speed not safety. An automobile for thrills, not seat-belts. The hills were barren, the sunshine was blinding, the car was an escape from reality. Suddenly I was an Italian Formula One race driver.

I descended toward the American airbase at Comiso, near the coast of southern Sicily. Pulling up to the gate, I showed my ID card to the guard and pointed my Italian rocket toward the base medical clinic.

Joe, the lieutenant I was sent to help out, was a young Polish-American kid from New Jersey. We spent the afternoon going over his files, then at quitting time he said, "Would you like to go out for dinner tonight with my fiancé and me?"

"Sure."

An hour later we drove into town. It looked like Beirut. Broken-down apartments and office buildings. One stoplight in the whole town, and it didn't work. We drove up a dark street and stopped in front of a small shop.

Joe said, "Come on. I want you to meet my future mother-in-law."

We entered what was obviously a bridal store, full of all the accessories of weddings. A middle-aged woman with those same luminous eyes that are standard issue in the Mediterranean world stood behind the counter.

Joe began to rattle off Italian like a machine gun. The woman's face lit up. It didn't matter whether she was twenty, forty or sixty years old. That face was beautiful, full of life. Joe told her I was sent to help him out in the office. She walked around the counter, engulfed me with her large arms and even more ample bosom, planted kisses on both cheeks, then spun and grabbed two porcelain figurines from the shelf. She presented them to me along with more kisses.

Stunned, I stood there with the two small statues while Joe and the lady spouted the native language back and forth to one another. But it wasn't quite Italian. This young American who had been here for less than a year was speaking the Sicilian version of Italian, and doing so fluently.

The door of the shop opened and a short, fierce looking man with a salt and pepper mustache walked in. Joe introduced him as his future father-in-law. He was as reserved and scary looking as the wife was outgoing and inviting. We said our polite good-byes and departed. As we went out the door, Joe grumbled as he glanced at my porcelain gifts. "I'm engaged to her daughter, and she's never given me anything!"

We drove through the gloomy streets to the edge of town and pointed the car toward the coast. We wound down a dark curving road until it came to the water. Our auto turned right and drove along the sea, dark waves rhythmically beating against the shore, moonlight tracing the tops of the waves.

After a few miles, a brightly lit restaurant appeared by the road, and we pulled into the gravel parking lot.

Standing at the bar, halfway through our first glass of wine, I sensed excitement at the door. In burst three natives, two girls and a young man. I was introduced to Joe's fiancé, her older brother and his wife.

We enjoyed a delightful dinner overlooking the sea. I didn't understand most of the conversation, but I did understand happiness, warm smiles, camaraderie, good food and fine wine. I found myself studying the young man and thinking about his parents, the wedding store owner and her fierce looking husband. Young Giuseppe had the endearing attitude and open-handed love of life that I had seen in the mother, and I wondered how long until he grew fierce and powerful like his father. I suspected it was inevitable.

In his great work, "The Italians," Luigi Barzini notes that the key to understanding Italy is realizing that the exercise of personal power through allegiances is the lifeblood of this culture. Seemingly bizarre things happen every day with no apparent logical explanation precisely because the reasons are not logical; they are the result of balances of power. In Sicily more than any other region of Italy, personal influence is the key element in survival and prosperity.

This power is acquired, weighed out and transmitted through the church, through friends, through marriages, through the workplace, but most of all, fundamentally through the family. Every human being is a constantly adjusting balancing-scale, weighing power from the simplest transactions of the marketplace on up to the offices of prime minister and pope. Every Italian is a gymnast walking a balance beam of personal power, and the most successful ones are like Olympic gold medalists.

When foreigners come to Italy they are generally enthralled by the Italian love of life. They find Italians vibrant, alive, engaged in the joy of living. There are many reasons for this exhilaration, but an unexpected one is simply this constant quest for power. Italians are in a process of continual assessment, evaluating every person and every life situation to maintain their position and balance in the world. They do it with good humor, with generosity, with a kind spirit, with an attitude that makes every person believe he or she is important when interacting with them. Human beings are infinitely important because interpersonal relationships are the essence of survival.

When an Italian converses with you, his eyes bore into yours like searchlights. He wants to see your heart, and he's measuring you. When older foreign men find beautiful young Italian women beaming into their middle-aged faces, they naively think those young females are attracted to them. Hardly. They are simply engaged in life and conversation with an energy and earnestness that half-alive souls from other countries have never experienced. Real life is very attractive, and this kind of vitality is Italy's greatest resource.

The evening broke up and the three Sicilians departed. Joe and I went to the bar and ordered a *digestivo*. Such a great word for the Italian benediction to a fine meal. You finish your dinner with a sense of fellowship, leaning across the bar, convincing yourself that this heady alcoholic drink is somehow aiding your "digestion." What it definitely does is cement your fellowship with your companions.

Joe and I drove (very carefully) back towards town and pulled into the central square, a dark, stone-floored, open-air social arena, people milling around. At night in Sicily I always had the sensation I was in a cave. There was little illumination either from street lights or the upper stories of buildings. Hard-core energy conservation. With few tall trees, on a moonless night the darkness above was thick and uninterrupted. There was just enough light for ground level only, like we were actors on a long continuous stage. We walked into the main bar in the piazza, had another glass of wine, and I watched my new friend talk to one native after another with all the naturalness of someone born and raised in Sicily. He was already one of them.

As we strolled back to our car Joe detoured past a large apartment building, and magically his fiancé appeared, all smiles, outside the main entrance. We spent a few minutes in conversation, then Joe and I headed back toward our automobile.

Casually I asked, "Joe, how old is your fiancé?"

"Sixteen."

I paused. "And you're going to take that young girl, who doesn't speak English, back to the states with you?"

"No. I'm staying here."

"You're staying here?"

"Yeah."

"What are you going to do?"

"I'm going to go to work for her father."

"Oh." I said. "What's his business?"

"He has a vineyard."

I stopped in the middle of the sidewalk. "You're going to go to work in his vineyard?"

I stared at him. "How big is the vineyard?"

"Well, last year he made two million."

"Oh," I looked down and started walking again. "I see."

The next morning was Saturday, and Joe and I drove to the seaside town of Gela on the southern coast of the island. I was anxious to see it.

During World War II my father made the invasion of Sicily at Gela with General Patton's army. Dad was an infantry sergeant, drafted into the war at the age of twenty-three. He was an initial replacement in the North African campaign, made the invasion of Sicily, then the D-Day invasion at Normandy, fought across France, was captured, then spent the last six months of the war in a prison in Poland. In three and a half years, he certainly had a very different military experience than my peacetime career.

Dad was one of those traumatized WWII veterans who found it difficult to talk about the agony he experienced. He won a Bronze Star in Sicily, a Silver Star at Omaha Beach during the D-Day invasion, and a Purple Heart when he was bayoneted and captured in France.

My father was pulled out of a British convalescent hospital to make the D-Day invasion. He hit the shore at H-hour, Omaha Beach, Easy Red sector. Possibly the most dangerous and deadly spot during the war.

His was the second wave. Dad spared me the details of the first wave. Engineer battalion, 100% casualties. Dad's group survived partly by hiding under dead bodies in the water.

As his landing craft approached my father was pressed against the gangplank-type door that opened by contact with the shore underneath the craft. The winds were so bad that many boats full of troops were blown way off course. Only a few of the tanks made it ashore. Some tanks were especially equipped with long pipe-like "snorkels" that sprouted straight up from the passenger compartment. They were designed to be dropped out at sea, then travel across the sea floor to the beach. Dad said he didn't think any made it. Machine gun fire rattled back and forth across the metal gangplank my father was pressed up against. Suddenly there was a slight lull in the fire, the landing door fell open, and the GIs poured out into the water. Loaded with a 60 pound pack on his back, Sergeant Lundberg went out the opening and into the water. The weight he carried immediately dragged him under. When he bobbed to surface, it was a living hell. Many of the soldiers who were dropped further out never made it to shore. They drowned.

The most vivid and probably realistic picture of this moment is preserved in Steven Spielberg's excellent film "Saving Private Ryan." It depicts in gruesome detail, the carnage where the Rangers hit west of my Dad's position. Bloody Omaha was much worse.

My father and some of his buddies made it ashore as best they could. Several GIs in Dad's outfit were dispatched to assemble a Bangalore torpedo to blow a hole in the concertina wire lying across the beach, blocking them from moving inland. Concertina is barbed wire strung in huge circles, hence the name "concertina," like a large circular accordion.

The Bangalore torpedo is aptly described by screenwriter and director Samuel Fuller, a veteran of D-Day. "The Bangalore Torpedo was 50 feet long and packed with 85 pounds of TNT, and you assembled it along the way - by hand. I'd love to meet the asshole who invented it!" It must have been put to serious use at D-Day because the four films that graphically show its use all center on the Normandy invasion: *Saving Private Ryan, The Longest Day, Storming Juno,* and *The Big Red One* (the nickname for my father's famous unit, The First Infantry Division).

The soldier who shoved the last section of torpedo under the barbed wire got himself entangled in the concertina. The lieutenant in charge of my father's outfit looked at Dad and said, "Lundberg, go get him out of there!"

Under deadly fire, Sergeant Lundberg made his way to the trapped GI, got him free and dragged him back to relative safety. For that my father received the Silver Star.

The Bangalore worked. It blew a hole in the wire, my father and his buddies surged through and survived D-Day.

They fought across France. At some point along the way, Dad and his men were dug into position in front of the enemy forces. The Germans started a counter-offensive and my father's position was overrun. Enemy soldiers streamed down on top of the American GIs who were partly hidden in the "foxholes."

Dad said, "The only thing I could do was grab the first soldier." He jumped out of the ditch, grabbed the German's rifle by the bayoneted end and tried to struggle him to the ground. The bayonet sliced open my father's hand and the other soldier hit my Dad over the head with a "potato masher," one of the large German hand grenades.

They marched him and the other captives through a French village toward an interrogation area. Mortar shells were flying over their heads, and by this time my father could sense the closeness of the missiles above. One shot whistled loudly, and all the prisoners instinctively hit the ground. The German guard never flinched.

"Get up!" he barked.

As they marched along, Dad looked at the German and said, "You speak good English."

"We have schools."

The prisoners were herded into a building and the questioning began. My father was led into a room where a German officer said, "Tell me what you know about the troop movements." Dad gave them his name, rank and serial number. The German pulled out his pistol and stuck it into my father's belly. Dad told me that he thought that was the end.

Thirty days later he was released from solitary confinement and ushered back to a cell with other American,

British and French soldiers. My father was the only one still in his uniform. The others were all wearing local civilian clothing.

Dad asked, "How long have you been here?"

"Oh, they released us right away, but they took our clothes."

Dad's comment to me was, "I guess they spilled their guts." The Germans later used those uniforms to infiltrate the American lines.

From there my father and the prisoners were put on trains and moved to the German/Polish border, Frankfurt on the Oder River. On the way the railroad was strafed by P-38 Lockheed Lightnings, the double-tailed American fighter planes. In warfare if the enemy didn't kill you, your comrades might.

When he hit the beaches at Normandy my father weighed two hundred pounds. When he was freed from the prison camp in Poland after six months confinement, he weighed 130 with dysentery.

Dad told me a few stories about the prison camp. He said that the first order of business every morning was to go through your clothes and kill all the lice by pinching them between your thumbnails. Next morning, same procedure.

He was imprisoned with a young German-American from Iowa who naturally received a great deal of harassment from the guards. "You are fighting against your own country!"

One day my father's friend simply walked out of the camp, speaking German. As he was making his way through town the air raid siren rang, and he was ushered into a shelter with the local civilians. They noticed his shaved head, emaciated appearance and strange clothing. He was escorted back to the prison camp with typical German efficiency.

Dad said the most religious of the prisoners were the Russians. "They were the only ones who set up their own sanctuary and held regular services."

Eventually the camp was liberated from the east by the advancing Russian army. When they took the camp they separated the prisoners from the German guards, who by this time in the late stages of the war were all old men and teenage boys. The Russians put all the prisoners to one side and all the guards on the other side. They killed every German.

As a child when I pushed my father to talk about the campaign in Sicily, he said it was pure hell, "29 days and nights of constant fighting."

After they came ashore at Gela, Dad said they lay in an almond grove, reaching up and grabbing nuts above their heads. That was the sanitized version of the story. Joe and I walked the beach, now absent of almond trees, covered with plastic tents covering rows of tomato plants. Up the slopes from the water, the barren hills still sprout old concrete "pillboxes," small mushroom-like structures from which German machine guns poured fire down on the invading GIs.

The Americans were sitting ducks, extremely lucky to have the almond groves giving partial shelter. My father told me two stories from Sicily.

"There was a Native American in my outfit named Olson. How he got that name, I don't know. If that man ever had fear, he never showed it. One night we moved up a hill under heavy German fire, and we were beaten back down. We got to the bottom of the hill, scared shitless, and Olson cocked his rifle, looked at us and said, 'Let's go get those sons-a-bitches.' We took the hill."

"Some time later, one night Olson said, 'Today is my 21st birthday, and I'm going to have a drink.' He had enlisted in the U.S. Army illegally when he was sixteen, now a five year veteran. The young lieutenant looked at Olson and said, 'You take a drink and you're busted.'"

"Of course Olson took the drink and was busted and another lieutenant in another company heard about it and picked Olson up for duty in his outfit."

My father, the son of Swedish immigrants, fell prey to the traditional curse of foreigners in Sicily. The same enemy that wiped out the brother of Queen Constance and her five hundred northern European knights, the same culprit who delayed Frederick from departing on the Crusade. Disease.

Dad contracted malaria. But before he was medically evacuated to Britain, Sergeant Lundberg and one of his fellow GIs, a Sicilian-American, visited that young man's grandmother, still living on the local family farm.

When Grandma realized who the olive-skinned American standing before her was, she threw her arms around him and said, "The farm is yours!" Shocked, he looked at her and replied, "You can keep it!"

Castle Building in Italy

Frederick continued to build up his kingdom and provided himself a lavish lifestyle. He enjoyed his falcons, his hunting and his harem. Extensive irrigation systems supported the prosperous farming industry.

Although Sicily was his natural home, Frederick had a great passion for southern Italy. He built marvelous castles all over the Puglia countryside. His court was constantly on the move, transported by an exotic caravan including camels, elephants, giraffes, and draped Middle Eastern divans, shaded by curtains and tended by huge black eunuchs, the guardians of his harem.

Frederick imported leopards, cheetahs and other animals for display and hunting. To this day in museums across modern Italy you discover old paintings showing these wild cats perched in cages behind riders on horseback, ready for the hunt.

His southern Italian fortresses were often located out in the countryside at scenic locations overlooking the forests and fields.

Frederick's castles teemed with festive life and young people drawn to his court. Volumes of books on multitudes of subjects filled his libraries. His own poetry and that of his court reflect the brilliant influence of the Middle East combined with the philosophy of Medieval European courtly love.

At his core Frederick was basically a highly intelligent seeker of truth ... and a loner. Growing up a virtual orphan, he wasn't much of a family man in the beginning. He simply didn't know how. He was exceedingly tolerant intellectually, interested in the knowledge of Christians, Moslems, Jews and the ancients. But he wasn't skilled in knowing whom to trust. And that was one element in his downfall.

Trouble was always brewing and Frederick's famous luck was about to change. After the kingdom felt secure, he led his army north to consolidate his larger vision. Frederick saw the future, an Italy united under a Holy Roman Emperor with large portions of Europe tacked on. It was not to be. Despite his genius, charisma, courage and supreme organizational skills, he had too many opponents.

Foremost were the popes. Frederick envisioned Rome as his capital. During his lifetime nearly all the popes he faced used every scheme at their disposal to impede and frustrate Frederick's ambitions. The Lombard city-states of the north wanted no ruler to trample their sovereignty, and the popes backed them. Germany was left in the charge of Frederick's first son Henry, another boy-king. He fell under the influence of ambitious advisors and turned against his father. Eventually Frederick re-entered Germany, then defeated and imprisoned Henry. But the damage was done.

Several more years remained on the first treaty the emperor had forged in the Holy Land. But the pope issued a call for another Crusade, an obvious ploy to lure Frederick far away. He bluntly refused.

Regaining the allegiance of the German nobles, he organized an army and marched south into Italy. Frederick was a good general, but his military forces were always pitifully small for his grand purposes. Throughout the summer of 1237 the army of Milan played cat and mouse with Frederick's forces. Finally in November he soundly defeated the Milanese, but he made a fatal mistake. Half the enemy army survived and slipped away. Frederick declined to pursue and finish them off.

The emperor spent the winter in northern Italy, resting and planning his next move. Only six northern Italian cities stood against him. Milan was the key.

The path to Milan was barred by the city of Brescia, half-way between Lake Iseo and Lake Garda. Frederick began his attack in July, and here the emperor's famous luck gave out. His brilliant engineer of siege machines was captured by the Brescians and went to work against him. The city stubbornly held out against the imperial army. Frustrated, Frederick sent a trusted emissary to negotiate for peace. The envoy turned traitor and urged the Brescians to delay. Frederick laid siege to the city.

The weather turned bad and he gave up the siege. A huge mistake. The legend of Frederick's invincibility was broken, and back in Rome the pope sensed weakness. He secretly convinced the powerful city-states of Genoa and Venice to turn against Frederick. Rumors spread of a pending excommunication of the emperor. Frederick spent the winter in Padua, near the mouth of the Po River.

Northern Italy

The broad plain of the Po River cuts from east to west across the northern part of Italy, providing an unusual flat avenue in an otherwise very mountainous country. This is the path Frederick took marching his army toward Brescia with Milan as his ultimate destination.

Today an autostrada funnels cars and trucks along the same route. In the years I lived in northern Italy, I often drove my BMW along this highway, quickly becoming "acculturated" to Italian motoring. There were no posted speed limits in those days. If the vehicle directly in front of you was moving too slowly for your taste, you simply moved into the outside lane and sped past it. If you lingered too long in the "fast lane" and a speedy car moved up behind you, he simply flashed his headlights and you quickly moved right to allow him to zoom past. It was very efficient ... and really quite safe because everyone understood the code of the road, and the drivers were very much "in tune" with one other. American GIs sent to Italy had a high accident rate, particularly their first year in the country. This was because they tried to drive like Italians without first understanding the ground rules.

Speed was the creed. All motorists yielded to the supreme variable in Italian driving, ... velocity. The rules were intuitive, understood by everyone, and written nowhere. Written regulations existed mostly for show.

And basically, all of Italy runs the same way. There are layers upon layers of bureaucratic regulations, administered by government employees who are infamous for their inefficiency and indifference. This bureaucracy provides a civilized framework for a country that has always functioned on interpersonal power and understanding.

During the years I lived in Italy my favorite business trip was the yearly visit I made to a small American communications site near Brescia. It lay a few miles south of Lake Garda.

I usually stayed in a simple hotel near Desenzano on the southern shore of the lake. The albergo was run by a retired Italian air force colonel from Sicily who had married a local woman and together they now ran this hotel. The rooms were simple and comfortable, and the adjoining restaurant was typical. The setting was simple, and the food was delicious. My favorite dish was the "Spaghetti Siciliana," and of course this endeared me to my Sicilian proprietor.

My contact at the communications site was a Puerto Rican, Sergeant Rodriquez. He was a wonderful host. After I finished my inspection, he and I would spend our evenings roaming the cobblestone streets of Desenzano. For me it was the perfect Italian town. Not too large, right on the water, full of a nice mixture of tourists and locals. It seemed Rodriquez knew everyone. He certainly knew the owner of every bar.

People like Rodriquez amaze me. They have the ability to speak more than one language fluently, and as soon as they learn the second tongue, it is a simple matter to move on to language 3, then language 4, and so on. These folks switch language channels as if they are human television sets.

Rodriquez was like that. We moved through the streets and alleys of Desenzano, and we visited every wine bar in town. Rodriquez knew the locals on a first-name basis, and he changed languages with push-button ease. From English to Italian to local dialect and back again. He might have even spoken Spanish at one time or another. It was a delight to watch him. The local wine was good too.

One evening we entered our first bar and as soon as we passed through the door, Rodriquez grabbed my arm and said,

"Major, do you see that man over there?" He nodded toward a middle-aged gentleman with salt and pepper mustache, wearing a sport-coat with an open collar, talking to the bartender.

"Yes."

"He's a local politician. I've seen him order half a dozen bottles of wine, one after another, pour them all out, until he gets one he likes."

I smiled, thinking that at these prices, it was worth the show.

At the next bar, Rodriquez launched into an extended conversation with a young, thin, unkept man with glazed eyes and dark hair. I couldn't understand their conversation so I just enjoyed the sights inside the bar.

As we left I asked, "Who was that guy?"

"Oh, he's a violin maker from Cremona." Obviously the town of Stradivarius, Guarnerius, and Amati still carried on its tradition.

Toward the end of the evening we entered a bar far down a dark side alley. This was a different sort of place. All the patrons were older men. Four of them sat at a small table, waves of glowing cigarette smoke drifting between them as they threw cards on the table in each other's direction. Rodriquez moved to the table.

As he talked to one of the players a young girl, perhaps eight years old approached the table and interrupted the conversation. All activity stopped and all eyes focused on this miniature person who spoke to her grandfather with complete assurance.

Yes, it's true. In Italy children are God.

The little girl departed and someone placed a case of wine beside Grandpa. The bottles were white wine, unlabeled.

I looked at Rodriquez. "What's up with the wine."

"It's what we're drinking. That's a local variety, private vineyard. It's called Lugana."

"Can I get half a case?"

"I'll find out."

Rodriquez went to talk to the barmaid. I watched the card game. In a few minutes he returned.

"I got you the wine. Let's go."

I wasn't disappointed.

Lake Garda is one of the top three windsurfing spots in Europe, along with Tarife in Spain and Lefkas, Greece. In summer, surfboards with colorful sails fill the lake. They buzz around on the water, framed by shores lined with palm trees. Garda has a wonderful microclimate, orange trees growing at the same latitude as Bangor, Maine.

On one of my last visits to Desenzano del Garda, my wife and I stayed in that favorite hotel. We walked into town, and the ancient cobblestone streets I loved were lined with dozens of Ferraris, some sort of sports car convention. Sleek futuristic autos in those brilliant Tuscan blues, forest greens, and glaring yellows you see in the Etruscan tomb paintings. The vehicles rested on those ancient brown stones like spaceships landing in a time warp in Medieval Europe.

There is no end to the ways Italy is a time machine.

*****

In the spring of 1239 the pope tightened the noose. He declared the excommunication (for the second time) of Frederick II, Emperor of the Holy Roman Empire. This sent a chill through northern Italy.

Various reasons were stated. Of course the real issue, an obvious power struggle between pope and emperor was left unspoken. At first Frederick accepted the news with the dignity of a king. But as the full fury of the pope's hatred of the emperor gushed out, Frederick responded in kind. The pope denounced him as a heretic who adopted Moslem customs like keeping a harem and bathing every day. The emperor proclaimed the pope an antichrist.

Underneath it all was a contest between two strong men each of whom saw himself as the Lord's anointed. The pope was the duly selected successor to St. Peter, guardian of Christianity. Since childhood Frederick bore the conviction he was God's chosen one, destined to rule the world as divine emperor. He saw the pope usurping secular power.

Northern Europe backed Frederick. The pope tried to bribe German princes with offers of land for their support. Generally they refused. Britain sided with Frederick who had taken an English princess as his third wife. Far away from the allegiance of Italian culture, northern Europe looked to the future.

The entire drama and the future of Europe hinged on Rome. The city was divided and confused, not knowing whether to support their "first bishop" or the emperor. Amazingly, the ninety-year-old pope led a procession through the streets, called on his fellow Romans to follow, and they rallied around him. Rather than forward, Rome looked back to the Middle Ages. The Church prevailed.

Discouraged, Frederick returned to southern Italy. As the months passed, support for the emperor poured in from Europe. German and British princes pressured Rome. Frederick regained his famous will and launched a series of military campaigns against Italian forces loyal to the pope. In some cases he won stunning victories, in others he was stalemated.

The emperor pointed his army toward Rome, devastating the countryside on a march to the eternal city. His army perched on the outskirts of the city, the future of Europe once again hung in the balance … and the pope died.

Suddenly Frederick had no opponent. Again he was blocked. At the same time Mongol hordes led by the son of Genghis Khan bore down on northern Europe with horrendous ferocity. The Holy Roman Emperor belonged in Germany leading the defense of his empire. But without papal support, Frederick was stuck in Italy. He awaited the election of a new pope.

Two years dragged by until a pope was selected. Innocent IV came from an old, established family of Genoa. Frederick happily began negotiations for a meeting of reconciliation with the new pontiff.

As the time of the meeting grew near, the pope secretly slipped away to Genoa, then proceeded to Lyons in France where he set up court. Frederick was furious and continued military skirmishes in Italy. The pope called a council in France and dismissed Frederick as emperor.

Enraged, Frederick and pope jockeyed for support with various European parties. The emperor made concessions that revealed his growing weakness. One of Frederick's problems was that he simply could not kill a pontiff. The opposite was not true. Fostered by the pope, an extensive secret plot grew to assassinate the emperor. Trusted allies and members of Frederick's court were implicated.

Frederick discovered the plan, then tortured and executed those involved. Heavily in debt he squandered his resources in fruitless military campaigns. He taxed southern Italy and Sicily while intrigue swirled all around him. Growing paranoid, he imprisoned, tortured and blinded some of his closest advisors.

It was a downward spiral. Finally, the wonder of the world retreated south, a spent man. Sick with dysentery, he clothed himself in the white robe of a Cistercian monk and died. He was buried with great honors in the cathedral in Palermo, where it all began.

Frederick was a flaming missile who shot across the Mediterranean world at the height of papal power. He never achieved his vision of a revived Roman Empire or a united Italy, but on his dream the future of Europe turned.

There would be ups and downs, but from this point forward the Catholic Church began a long decline in secular power. The die was cast, but it was another five hundred years before the pope gave up the Papal States and retreated to the Vatican, until Italy was finally united.

Frederick died in 1250. Fifteen years later a child was born in northern Italy. Just as brilliant as Frederick, he saw the same future. A devout Christian, he fought the popes from north of Rome just as his predecessor had battled from the south. He propelled Italy in the same inevitable direction, not with armies but with something more durable, the written word.

Another Miraculous Birth

In the year 1265 A.D., fifteen years after the death of Frederick II, a male child was born into an Italian family of average nobility, prominence and wealth. The child grew into a person of mediocre build, appearance and demeanor. However, nothing else about him or his world was commonplace.

As a youngster it was apparent he possessed a special intellect. As the years went by he displayed deep convictions, great diplomatic ability and singular leadership. He became a brave soldier, a passionate lover, a stunning orator and a leading politician. He lived in the emerging, greatest city of Europe, and he was its most prominent, devoted and controversial citizen. In the end he became the greatest writer in Italian history ... and an outcast.

In the thirteenth century his city was the second largest in Europe and the strongest financially. Within a short time after its gold coin was introduced, that coin became the dominant currency on the entire continent. Within 200 years this city's art and culture achieved levels that have never been surpassed. Today its museums and churches hold more great art per square foot than any other city in the world.

In this contentious, intellectual and artistic environment, the seed of "cultural rebirth" was planted with passion, nourished with strong finances and tended with intellectual love of the arts. Christianity was a dominant and conflicting force, continuing as an inherent part of Italian and European life. This city and this man led the way into the period of history we know as the Renaissance. Together they gave birth to our modern world.

The city was Florence, the coin was the gold florin, and the man was Dante Alighieri. This is his story.

Campaldino, Tuscany

The great warhorse shuddered in the chill, early morning air. Across the flat valley dull, gray morning light crept over the horizon and flowed over dark figures on horseback, a long silhouetted line stretching from north to south. Small puffs of morning fog rose like ghosts from the cold ground.

Sensing tension, the warhorse bolted forward, and Dante reined him in, leaning close to the neck, "Easy, great one, easy." He quickly brought his mount back into line.

On both sides of Dante, armored warriors were lined up on similar horses, steam puffing from the mouths of both men and beasts. The two lines faced one another, less than two hundred meters apart.

The rider on Dante's left turned his head, white teeth flashing. "You handle him well, Florentine."

"He is a good horse."

"Does he have a good rider?"

"Yes."

"A good swordsman?"

"Fair."

The line of teeth widened. "I am better with the sword than with the horse. Stay close to me, Florentine. Maybe we will both live."

Dante glanced sideways, then back toward the enemy. The other man spoke again.

"Are you the one they call The Poet?"

"I have been called that."

The rider turned and leaned right extending his arm. "Bernadino da Polenta."

Dante grasped the gloved hand. "Dante Alighieri," he replied. "You are not Florentine."

"Ravenna."

"Guido da Polenta is the ruler of Ravenna."

"My father," he said. "Tell me Poet, which side will win the day?"

"We outnumber them, but those of Arezzo are good men and good fighters. God knows."

"But he is not saying much at the moment."

Dante turned and smiled. "He will speak by the end of the day."

From their right, three men rode along the line of cavalry, slowing as they neared the center of the line. They spun their horses to face their comrades, the crest of Florence showing on each man's chest.

Da Polenta glanced a questioning look toward Dante.

"Vieri de Cerchi," the Florentine whispered.

The center rider was older, more solid that the young men to his right and left, his face lined and proud. He urged his horse forward a step.

"Men of Florence, comrades, defenders of the Church, Guelph warriors. Today we face a proud imperial opponent. The men of Arezzo follow the emperor. Our allegiance is first with the church and our pope. It is my sacred duty to pick twelve warriors to stand in the forefront of battle."

Silence followed. De Cerchi was much admired in Florence, active in the city council, from a proud and well-established noble family. His choice would bestow honor on any chosen, also serious danger for the twelve men at the apex of the attack.

De Cerchi raised his chin another notch. "I choose my two sons, my three nephews and myself. We will stand in the breech. I ask for six more volunteers from the noble men of Florence."

A murmur swept across the line. Dante smiled, and his eyes glistened. Under no compulsion to do so, De Cerchi had placed his family in the first line of battle. Just as impressive, De Cerchi was not physically the best choice; he was lame in one leg.

Voices on horseback began to swell. Dante urged his great horse forward a step. "I volunteer. Dante Alighieri."

The older man faced Dante and replied, *"Bravo, Alighieri.* You are young; you back up the twelve."

"Si, Signor."

Quickly other men voiced their desire to serve among the twelve. After over twenty volunteers, De Cerchi raised his arm. *"Basta."* "Enough. You Florentines have quit yourselves like men. Our forefront will be twenty horsemen. Our strict orders are to allow the Aretines to attack first. We hold our ground until they are upon us. Watch for my signal to engage. God be with you."

De Cerchi turned his horse to face the opposition, and ten cavalry lined up on each side of him.

Dante maneuvered his horse just behind the front line. Da Polenta stayed beside him. "I do not like this, Poet. If we wait, their cavalry will smash right through us."

"Our commander Mangiadori has his reasons."

"I don't care about his reasons. I would like to be alive at sunset."

"Mangiadori is wise and battle tested. Trust in that."

"Well, Alighieri, I hear you are a religious man. I hope God is on our side."

"He is not."

"What? We represent the Guelphs, the party of Church and pope."

Dante turned. "Those facing us are good men, Christian men. I do not believe God takes sides when good men oppose one another. The Almighty is not our servant."

Da Polenta did not reply, but his eyes held Dante's face for a long moment.

Suddenly, a lone trumpet blast pierced the damp air, coming from the line of Arezzo cavalry. A low rumble began as the horizon of mounted horsemen trembled. The sound grew as the long, dark silhouette shook and thundered toward the waiting Florentines. Tension surged across Dante's line, and his comrades struggled to hold their horses in position.

Lined on both sides of old De Cerchi, the riders ahead of Dante moved forward, circling and shielding the lame knight. The commander raised his sword, and his deep voice split the air, "Hold fast. Hold!"

The enemy horsemen avalanched toward Dante's line, dust billowing around them, obscuring the horses. The pounding of hoofs swelled.

"Poet, they will crush us!" Da Polenta screamed. Dante raised his sword and clenched his teeth.

The enemy line bore down, swords flashing in morning light, when thirty meters apart, De Cerchi screamed, "Charge!"

The command was barely heard above the earthquake of attack; the Florentine line began to move forward into the collision.

The enemy hit like a freight train. Horses, men and steel colliding. Knights and mounts screaming, metal clanging in a cloud of impenetrable dust. Florentine knights were knocked from their horses, swords flashed downward slicing arms and necks of thrown men.

Dante sensed movement from ahead and his right; an enemy horseman came at him, sword raised. At the last second Dante swung his horse to the right, ramming the other animal, knocking the knight off balance as his sword came down and glanced off Dante's shield. The Aretine collided into Da Polenta, and both were thrown from their mounts. Da Polenta came up quickly, lunged toward the knight, his sword plunging into the man's throat. Blood gushed on both sides of the weapon.

Another mounted knight bore down on Da Polenta, vulnerable now on foot. Dante charged at the attacker, and distracted, the other horsemen turned to engage Dante. A long lance lay nearby, next to a dying horse. Da Polenta seized it, and as the Aretine brought his sword down on Dante's shield, Da Polenta plunged the lance into the horse's underbelly. The horse screamed, reared and twisted, coming down on its side, pinning the knight to the ground. Da Polenta quickly killed the stricken man before he could get free.

Three short trumpet blasts blared. The signal for retreat.

Da Polenta ran to Dante's horse, lifted his arm, and the Florentine hoisted him up on the back of the saddle.

"Let's go, Poet! To the rear!"

"We cannot retreat!"

"Follow orders, Dante. This is not over!"

Dante swung his horse and headed back, swerving around fallen horses, dead and moaning men, and some still fighting.

To the rear of the main battle, Corso Donati, a Florentine, commanded a contingent of cavalry from Pistoia. Donati was under strict orders to hold fast until ordered, but he saw the Florentine cavalry being routed, and he was not a man to follow orders well.

He turned and shouted, "Men of Pistoia, if we lose, I will die in battle with my fellow citizens. And if we conquer, let any man come to Pistoia to punish us." With that he raised his sword. "Follow me!"

Donati spurred his horse and swept around other waiting groups of horsemen, approaching the battle from the right rear. Gaining speed, his men behind him, they closed on the right flank where the Florentines were struggling just to stay alive, and inching backward. The Pistoians struck hard, surprising the Aretines from the side, and the momentum of the enemy stalled as Donati's men engaged in battle.

Da Polenta hung on as Dante maneuvered through the chaos. Glancing back he watched Donati's men hit the flank. A single long trumpet blast sounded from the Florentine side.

He leaned forward and shouted in Dante's ear, "Turn around, Poet, we're back in this!"

Dante swung his horse around and hesitated. "Bernadino, there are free horses all around. Do you want one?"

"I do not ride a strange horse. I stay with you. Work the horse, I shall work the sword." Grinning widely, "Like I said, together we might even survive."

Spurring his mount, Dante moved toward an Aretine battling one of Donati's men. Approaching from the enemy's blind side, the Poet swung close and Da Polenta brought his blade down hard on the back of the man's neck. The body went slack and slid from the mount.

Another long trumpet blast and Dante swung to see Florentine foot soldiers on the run, entering the cavalry battle.

Da Polenta screamed, "We have them, Poet! The Aretine foot soldiers are too far away!"

The attackers were being overrun now. Completely outnumbered, Donati attacking from the flank, the resurgent Florentine line pushing back, foot soldiers entering the fray, the unity of the Aretine force melted.

The knights from Arezzo were now falling fast, and the Florentines were gaining new energy. The battle waged on for another hour, but it was over. Florence was triumphant.

One month later, Dante and Bernadino were sitting in a Florence piazza on a glorious summer afternoon, bathed in sunshine, sipping golden wine.

Da Polenta was in fine form, praising the wine, the beauty of Florentine women, and satisfaction in the recent victory. "My friend, we proved ourselves worthy of our alliance, routing the men of Arezzo, who I must admit acquitted themselves well, but we smashed them. In its own way that day was as glorious as today is beautiful."

He lifted his glass and glanced toward Alighieri. "What is the matter, Poet? You look melancholy. Perhaps one of your romances has soured?"

Dante shot his companion a wry look. *"Signor Ravenesi* (citizen of Ravenna), the whole episode, except our new friendship, was a disaster. You remember the night of the victory. Men acting like children, drinking and boasting of their superiority, glorying in spilled blood. The fact is we were fortunate to defeat a force of good men, half our size. Instead of pursuing the survivors to Arezzo and taking the city, we dallied and bragged and drank. Two weeks later, sobered up, we marched to Arezzo, ran a silly race around its walls, attacked the city to no result and burnt a few outlying farms. If that is victory with so many good men dying, I would hate to see how we define defeat."

"Alighieri, you are far too serious and melancholy. I fear it will be your undoing. Remember what life is all about. *La Pasta, La Donna, e Il Cavallo.* And remember, I am not good with horses, so you take care of the horses, and I will content myself with the other two."

Dante smiled, "I am slender, it is obvious that your one true gift is your undying love of good food, leave the women to those of us who have skill in love."

"Bah! You poets talk of love."

"But I notice that women listen."

"Then it is settled!" Da Polenta roared, reaching for the goblet and refilling both glasses, "You talk for both of us, I will tend to the wine!"

Dante lifted his glass. "Done!"

After a few moments, Bernadino spoke. "Tell me, Poet, do you have a special woman or are you a true democrat?"

The Florentine's face went blank and he looked away. "I have a special woman who I prize above all others. In fact, I think of her separately from all others."

Intrigued, Da Polenta said, "Well, that fits your serious nature. When were you last with her?"

"I have never been with her in that manner."

"What! What good is that?"

"She is the true love of my life. It is a love from the heavens, like an urgent thunderbolt that splits a man's chest, reaches inside, grabs the heart with the softest and strongest of fingers, incapable of release. I am a happy, helpless slave to such spiritual power."

Bernadino said softly, "Well you certainly have a way with words. How long have you known her?"

"Fifteen years, and every thought of her in that time has been pure delight."

"Fifteen years! You were a child."

"As was she."

"Her name?"

"You must vow not to repeat it."

"I will not."

"Beatrice Portinari."

"Florentine?"

"She is, as is her husband."

Da Polenta took another sip. "I see. This makes it more difficult. You must find a way to secretly begin a love affair."

Dante smiled. "I have a love affair with her, perhaps the greatest love a man can know. But I would never jeopardize this perfection for physical pleasure, nor would I risk her reputation."

His companion leaned back and exhaled slowly. "You are a strange one, Poet. I sense your life will be very difficult. Few men are crazy enough to be so noble. If you live mainly for principle, the world will chew you up and spit you out.

"Furthermore, your friends will desert you. Few are foolish enough to help a man who insists on falling on his own sword for the sake of lofty ideas."

"It is not only ideas or ideals I love, Bernadino. I love my city. Florence is the greatest city in the world. Our love of learning, our nobility, our patronage of the arts, our financial strength, our democratic heritage. Ravenna is also a fine city, but I was singularly blessed to be born in this place, in this time. In this world for me, it is the commune first!"

Florence

Florence was the first place my wife and I visited when we left Greece together. We decided to do our version of the grand European tour. Italy, Switzerland, Austria, France, Holland and Great Britain were on the itinerary. We picked one city in each country to give a picture of that culture. I lacked the benefit of a liberal education, but somehow Florence seemed the quintessential Italian place.

We landed in Rome, took an airport bus to the train station and caught the first departure for *"Firenze."* It rained the entire journey.

Those were the days, the late 1970s, when the American dollar was still king. It was embarrassing how little the comfortable pension in the center of Florence cost. Even worse, a continental breakfast of wonderful bread, jam and coffee was included. If real Italian bread was served in every country, there would be no need for cake. If authentic Italian cappuccino were served everywhere, there would be no reason for soup.

We roamed the rainy sidewalks. Under dark, round umbrellas businessmen scurried around us like nervous turtles. I met fellow Americans traveling alone, staying in first class hotels costing ten times what we paid. I felt sorry for them.

I bought leather gloves and artwork that I still have. Silk scarves on the Ponte Vecchio were a real bargain, but it was such an enchanted time I wouldn't have minded if they were severely overpriced. However, the real magic began when we stepped into the first museum.

Any visitor with no knowledge of Florence only has to encounter the art to realize that this city is unique in our world. The great thing about Florence is that the paintings and sculptures are divided into a series of museums. These separate buildings offer stunning but digestible chunks of great culture. You can relish them one at a time, and this has the advantage of not allowing you to be overwhelmed, although sometimes one painting seems enough for the whole day. I felt like a kid who discovered half a dozen candy stores all in a row. Why in college did I ever major in science and engineering?

The food is great everywhere in Italy. And it must be wonderful in Florence, but I have no memory of the restaurants. Here you live on art.

No picture of Michelangelo's David can do it justice. No movie with inspired dialogue delivered by a commentator with a deep, resonant voice can duplicate your first encounter with this living piece of marble. You walk into the room, and it becomes a secular sanctuary. The massive body stares down, and you look up to worship. You circle the stone and power radiates from it. It's as if you are standing still and David is slowly turning. Naked, but in total control. This is not a Hebrew youth coming of age at the moment he defeated Goliath; this is the western world in a superhuman body, being reborn in the glory of the Renaissance. If creativity is the essence of God, then artists like Michelangelo should be thankful every moment of their lives for the chance to mold masterpieces and mirror the divine.

At the Uffizi Gallery is Botticelli's "Birth of Venus." She rises from the sea, standing naked, un-self-conscious and supremely realistic. Like many great artists Botticelli added ironic twists. Venus supports her weight on the leg that is bent, not on the one that is straight. Impossible in this world, but not in the Renaissance, when all things seemed possible.

Wandering about, we came upon paintings by Michelangelo. They were easy to recognize. No one has ever painted with such supreme realism in regard to anatomy. Muscles bulge as in modern photographs of body-builders.

Michelangelo learned his craft by secretly and illegally dissecting corpses at night.

One of the plain truths of why Italy is so attractive is simply that it is so real. Michelangelo was compelled to find reality in sculpture and painting. He was driven to sneak into morgues to investigate flesh and blood. He painted and sculpted to release life when it was commonplace to distort reality by smoothing it out or hiding it under clothing. In one way or another, every other culture lacks Italian realism. French impressionism is beautiful, but it is distorted. English literature is full of flowery, unnecessary language. Politicians around the world gloss over, under and around the truth. Even Greek mosaics are unrealistic. Under the veneer of religion, at its core Italy is a country of the flesh. *La dolce vita* is not just sweet, it is raw and real. That is what makes Italian living great, … and so very attractive.

I sat in the main square, the Piazza della Signoria, and drank a beer served in a mug the size of a small aquarium. For the first time in my life I had no desire to move or leave this spot for the rest of the evening, the rest of the week. Who knows, maybe for the rest of my life?

I've written this book, and I've done my best to imagine what it was like for Dante. Blessed with extraordinary talent, cursed with banishment from his birthplace, the greatest city in Europe. Like most Italians, his life and heartbeat were imbedded in the stones and art of the place where he grew up. Twenty-five centuries after Ulysses, Dante's similar twenty year exile is a reflection of every person separated from what he loves.

The deeper the love, the greater the pain. And in Italy love and pain run very deep. As deep as life itself.

*****

Dante continued his conversation with Bernadino Da Polenta.

"But enough of me and my city for now. Tell me of the love of your family, my friend."

Da Polenta smiled broadly. "You know me, Poet. I am a young man of energy and good appetites. I enjoy good food, good wine, and good women." He paused. "But I like constant variety in all of them."

"I did not mean you, … I meant your sister."

Bernardino's smile faded, and he looked down toward the cobblestones of the piazza. "Surely you have heard the stories."

"I have, but I do not know which are true."

"And you think I will tell you the truth."

"Yes, I do."

"Well, my friend, you have been candid with me. I will be candid with you. But you must promise to be discreet about what I am about to say."

"You have my word."

Da Polenta took a long sip.

"My family has long been an ally of the Malatestis of Rimini. Both that city and Ravenna are aligned with the Guelphs, as is your fair city. About thirteen years ago, my father Guido arranged a marriage between my sister Francesca and Gianciotto de'Malatesti. The purpose of course, was to strengthen the bonds between our cities and families. Gianciotto's older brother Paul worked out the arrangement."

"Gianciotto is a fine warrior, and commands great respect. After his marriage he spent much time away from Rimini on diplomatic and other missions. Paul is married to his own cousin Orabile, who was once a prisoner of the

Montefeltros. Orabile is a bit older than Paul; they have two children."

"In any event, over the years with Gianciotto absent a great deal, Paul had free access to my sister, and well, one thing led to another, and they carried on a liaison. Eventually these affairs become known, Gianciotto was informed, and in a rage he burst in upon the lovers and killed them both."

Bernadino went silent.

"I am sorry for the loss of your sister," Dante said.

Both men slowly reached for their wine goblets.

*****

To understand medieval attitudes toward marriage, sex and love requires a bit of independent thought. Marriage in those times was almost always simply a business transaction arranged by the families, particularly so among the nobility. It had nothing to do with romantic love, although it had everything to do with the family. Life was treacherous and insecure, with constant conflict. Wise alliances and preservation of the family's assets were all important for survival. Many engagements were arranged between children by their parents. Marriage might be many years later. In Dante's own case he was betrothed to Gemma Donati at the age of twelve and married nine years later.

However, dispassionate marriage transactions did not dispel passion. In Dante's time the idea of the romantic troubadour was very much alive. Legends like that of Lancelot and Guinevere were all the rage. Dante's devoted spouse ignored his various love affairs.

Later, Dante included the story of Francesca, Paul and Gianciotto in his Divine Comedy. He idealized and romanticized the facts. And he placed Francesca in the most benign area of Hell. In other words, hers was a small sin. It seems obvious he also viewed his own personal romances as minor, or at least nearly irresistible.

Years later in Bologna Dante confided to his friend and fellow poet, Cino da Pistoia, "I have been with Love since I was nine years old, and I know how it pauses and rages, and how under its influence, one rejoices and moans. He who tries reasoning and virtue with Love is like someone who lifts his voice in a tempest."

A great man, Dante, but certainly like the rest of us, a very human one.

When we think in amusement, and hopefully a bit of tolerance, of the stereotype of Italians as passionate, gifted lovers who move deftly across marriage lines (and single lines), perhaps this is one more way that modern Italy becomes our time machine to the past. We begin to understand how it all came about … and how to some degree it continues.

*****

Da Polenta returned to Ravenna, and Dante resumed his life in Florence. His family grew, children were born to him and Gemma Donati. Our poet managed his family property, played with his children, enjoyed his writing and music. However, tragedy and loss loomed.

That winter the father of Beatrice died. Folco Portinari was a leading citizen of Florence, a good man and much admired. Dante composed poetic words of comfort for Beatrice's loss. Six months later Beatrice herself died suddenly, and Dante plunged into grief and sadness. His family and friends consoled him; he slowly pulled out of his depression and turned more and more to his writing.

His first major work was the *Vita Nuova,* New Life. It is a compilation of the poems he had previously written regarding Beatrice, along with others that related to his love for her. Dante linked these poems together with masterful prose, and the result is a short work of about one hundred pages. However, the quality of the work firmly cemented Dante's talent as a poet and to some degree as a writer.

The city of Florence was evolving with great turmoil into a leading city of Europe. It was a Guelph city, but at times in the past had been governed by the Ghibellines. In very broad terms the Guelphs were the party of the Church, which supported the idea of independent city-states. The Ghibellines were the party of the emperor. Someone has noted that one way to remember this difference is by way of syllables in the words. Guelph – Church (one syllable). Ghibelline – Emperor (multiple syllables). In truth, the factions within the two parties made this distinction unclear. In addition, the popes sided with first one party, then another, and as we shall see, at times with certain factions within a party. The idea on the church's part was that if no particular party gained real power, the church would continue with strong influence. Otherwise, the rise of strong, secular power would mean the certain demise of the Church's power and influence.

We saw this issue clearly in the life of Frederick II. Soon the same sort of power struggles would overwhelm Dante's life.

A clear example of this constant, confused jockeying for political power lies in the tragic story of Count Ugolino of Pisa.

Pisa was a Ghibelline city in name. The city leaders had stripped the nobility of any special powers beyond their wealth. The Guelph leaders had been expelled, and one of them, Ugolino, met with Guelph leaders in other Tuscan cities such as Florence. Enlisting these Guelph cities as allies, he attacked Pisa until it finally was so weakened that Ugolino and the Guelphs were allowed to reenter the city.

Ambitious and ruthless, Ugolino maneuvered to become the ultimate leader of Pisa. His political rivals were two of his relatives. He poisoned a young and charismatic cousin, but the count's grandson, Nino, was a more formidable competitor.

Grandfather and grandson challenged and fought each other for control. Finally, after a long struggle the count and Nino agreed to share power in Pisa. The archbishop of Pisa, Ruggieri (aligned with the Ghibellines), was just as ruthless and crafty as Ugolino, and the two of them plotted to drive Nino from the city. They succeeded. Nino fled.

The archbishop bided his time, and at the appropriate moment, incited the people against his partner Ugolino. The count with two of his sons and two grandsons was jailed in the upper portion of a tower. The keys of the tower were thrown in the river, and the prisoners were denied food. Eight months later Guelph forces retook the city, the tower was broken into, and the five starved bodies thrown into a common grave. Dante later embellishes the story in the Inferno portion of his Divine Comedy, placing Ugolino in a particularly nasty portion of Hell.

*****

Although it's a gruesome story (and there are several different versions, depending on which secret, backroom deals you believe), any of the variations is a classic example of Italian politics, both then and now.

Pisa, nominally a Ghibelline city, was actually in practice an evolving democratic one. It was attacked by Guelph forces (supposedly the party of church and the people) from surrounding cities that were allied with a Guelph leader (Ugolino) who obviously desired to be sole dictator of Pisa. The archbishop allied himself with the Ghibellines, rather than the Guelphs, and betrayed Ugolino. It would be hard to make this stuff up or to the outside observer, make it any more confusing.

During my lifetime the country of Italy has been famous for its "revolving governments." Rarely has one party held power at the national level for more than a year or two. Governments were constantly forming and collapsing, yet as always, Italy went on and even prospered. And generally the same people stayed in charge in slightly different roles. Only when a particularly brilliant politician, like a Mussolini or a Berlusconi, came to power could a government endure for years. And the genius of those types of leaders lay in that old Italian stand-by, … the expert use of personal power, … seasoned with great cunning, unlimited confidence, a sharp understanding of the national mood, and superb theatrical skills.

Once again, to understand today's Italy we must only look to its past. We must only travel through time.

*****

In Dante's Florence the "White" Guelphs represented the rising merchant class. The "Black" Guelphs represented the nobility. During the Poet's twenties, Corso Donati, one of the heroes of the battle of Campaldino, became leader of the Blacks.

Dante's emerging genius and talent were becoming obvious, and his family and friends urged him to enter political affairs. Many of his friends were aligned with the Whites.

Dante's life was marked by many personal losses. He continually lost friends and allies, often at strategic moments. Just before the battle of Campaldino when Dante was twenty-four years old, he met and became fast friends with a remarkable young man. Charles Martel was eighteen years old, the oldest son of Charles II, a Frenchman who had been named King of Naples. On his journey to his new appointment, Charles and his son passed through Florence. There were threats against the king's life so a force of 800 men accompanied Charles to Naples. Dante was part of this armed force.

He and the young prince became fast friends, sharing keen intellects and noble principles. Through the 1290s, as Dante matured, he was sent by the ruling council of Florence on at least fourteen diplomatic missions throughout Italy. Border disputes, alliances, pleading for condemned men and so on. He traveled to Genoa, Siena, Puglia and at least four times to the pope. Two missions were to Naples where he renewed and strengthened his friendship with young Charles Martel. Though still in his twenties, Dante became a highly skilled diplomat. His missions were very successful, and his reputation grew.

Martel was heir to the throne of Naples, the kingdom of Hungary and Sicily. Dante saw him as a good man, a fine friend, and ultimately someone who could possibly bridge the gap and unite the warring Guelph and Ghibelline factions.

Charles II and son Martel revisited Florence in 1294, and now a young crown prince in his twenties, he bestowed honors on Dante, and once again hope dawned for young Alighieri. Once again it was squashed.

Charles Martel and his wife died of the plague the very next year in Naples. Worse yet, Brunetto Latini, the widely respected Florentine scholar and diplomat, who had taken charge of the young poet's education after the death of his father, also died. Dante lived in an insecure and cruel world where death constantly lurked in the shadows behind war, disease and vendettas.

At the same time the church in Rome was in absolute turmoil.

Remember that at the death of Frederick II the popes began turning more and more to French kings for support rather than Frederick's Holy Roman Empire, which was Germany-based. This did not stop the church's political problems; it simply switched them from mostly German to mostly French.

The church was also desperate for money so all sorts of religious blessings and positions (like that of cardinal) were simply and shamelessly sold to the highest bidders. The last half of the thirteenth century (the late 1200s) saw a succession of thirteen different popes. Because of greatly increased support from France, more and more of the cardinals were French.

Finally in 1294, a papal conclave, deadlocked for two years, elected a monk, Celestine V as pope. It was a complete disaster to throw a totally unworldly man into this political cauldron. He abdicated after five months and was replaced by Boniface VIII.

Boniface was an ambitious, proud, aggressive and crafty lawyer-cleric. He was also ruthless. Boniface imprisoned the weak, aged former pope, and he died within a relatively short period of time. Boniface was elected pope at the same time Dante formally entered Florentine politics. In a world where politics and religion were so mixed together and turbulent, a violent collision loomed on the horizon between these two strong men.

All citizens of Florence were required to join one of the Guilds, and Dante enrolled in the Guild of Doctors and Druggists. Although he was neither of the two, this particular guild by tradition fit his position of both noble and poet, and it allowed him to formally enter politics.

By nature Dante was a quiet and serious person, but when he spoke, people listened. He was elegant, articulate, persuasive, forceful and brilliant. That helped. However, he was also noble, idealistic, stubborn, vain and naïve. That didn't.

Within a short time Dante was consulted by the Florentine government on all important business and began his highly successful diplomatic career. He was a rising star, and during his missions to the pope, Boniface took the measure of this young man.

When Dante's father died, Dante as the oldest son had become leader of the family and manager of business affairs. The family had rental property that provided income. In 1297, financial problems surfaced, and Dante was forced to take out a large loan. This added extra stress on the young man, who was descending more and more into the political quagmire that has always been Italy.

The year 1300 would be the great turning point of Dante's life. In fact, he centers his Divine Comedy on this year and its activities. It is the axis on which his life spins. It began with Florence sending Dante on a diplomatic mission to the majestic and powerful city-state of San Gimignano, twenty miles south of Florence.

San Gimignano

Driving up the Tuscan hill to the ancient city-state of San Gimignano is like approaching New York City in a submarine. Ascending in your auto, the ancient ramparts become visible as if your submarine is just breaking the surface of the water in the harbor. Suddenly medieval skyscrapers soar above you, sprouting straight up into the sky, each tower trying to outdo its neighbors like the great buildings of Manhattan. The skyline stabilizes, you park your car and enter a timeless world of cobblestone streets winding toward the center and crest of the town, which is the Duomo, the great cathedral.

Today fourteen towers remain. What it must have looked like in the days of Dante when seventy such fortresses competed with each other in prestige and defensive strength.

The first time I visited San Gimignano was in the 1980s, and I drove through endless fields of giant sunflowers whose large round, golden blossoms surrounded me on all sides. I felt like a small child wandering in some fairytale meadow full of flowers so large they seemed like playmates.

Today the fields have vanished. I guess some agricultural adjustment has deemed flower growing less profitable now. It is blazing hot, not a leaf stirring, and as my wife and I enter the gates, we are drawn to the first gelato shop, the coolness of its stainless steel display case pulling us magnetically toward it. Ice cream never tasted so good or melted so fast.

From outside the city the skyline of hundreds of years seems frozen in time. Inside, much is different from even my last visit of twenty years earlier. The shabby, dusty streets are paved with new cobblestones; the shops and ancient palaces lining the walkways look old-new, built in ancient style, recently refurbished. On my last visit, I wandered toward the center of town without encountering souvenir stores or sweetshops or coffee bars. Now much is commercial, euros are trading hands all around us.

Before, the central square held a non-working fountain, deserted except for a skinny mongrel dog and two young tourists in jeans, tee shirts and backpacks, posing as they took each other's photo in the blinding yellow light. Now the whole world seems to be here, the fountain is working, and the visitors are still taking pictures.

Years ago it was simple for us to find a small, cozy trattoria down one of the shaded alleyways, the stone interior providing natural cooling. It seemed like the only decent eating spot in town. Now there are numerous restaurants, each with elaborate facades and wooden placards propped outside proclaiming the daily specials in vivid, colored letters. I wouldn't know which one to choose. Before, it didn't even seem like a choice.

This small, great Tuscan commune was built magnificently to defend itself against the warring Guelphs and Ghibellines. Now it welcomes modern invaders to make a living.

*****

Florence in 1300 was bubbling with discontent, and Boniface clearly saw the city as a crown jewel of the Italian peninsula.

The Guelph party governing Florence had two main factions: the Whites and the Blacks. Corso Donati was leader of the Blacks. The DeCerchis and Guido Cavalcanti, a renowned poet, were leaders of the Whites. Cavalcanti was an older, trusted friend of Dante. In fact many years earlier the older Cavalcanti had been the one who sought out and discovered the identity of the young anonymous poet who had written the brilliant love sonnets to the "beautiful and virtuous young woman."

The turmoil in Florence centered on the conflict between the Whites, who were in power, and the Blacks, who wanted to be. The pope secretly intrigued with Donati and the Blacks to gain power over the city.

In April three citizens of Florence, allies of the pope, were denounced as conspirators and brought to trial. Boniface immediately sent orders to stop the trial. The orders were ignored.

The three men were ordered to pay a large fine. Boniface ordered the bishop of Florence to insist that the fine be annulled. Also ignored.

Boniface then sent a scathing letter demanding that the authors of the sentence against the three men must appear before the pope. Again ignored.

Boniface then excommunicated the entire city of Florence.

Matters were heating up.

The first of May was a festival day in Tuscany. That evening two parading groups chanced to meet in one of the main squares. One consisted of members of the Donati family, the other group were DeCerchis. A bloody brawl broke out.

Boniface soon heard of the disturbance. He immediately sent one of his respected cardinals to mediate with the idea that members of both parties should share governance of the city. The cardinal was received with respect, but the Whites rejected the idea of power-sharing with the Blacks.

One month later the annual election of ruling priors of Florence took place. Six leaders were chosen to lead the city. Five obscure men and the rising star of Florentine politics, thirty-five year old Dante Alighieri.

Bitter and enraged at being shut out of the government despite the cardinal's intervention, Donati and the Blacks continued to agitate, and they announced the coming arrival of a French prince who would set the city in order. The Whites took up arms, and Dante was forced to act.

He assembled the citizens of Florence around the main government building and announced the banishment from Florence of the main leaders and agitators of both the Blacks and the Whites.

The exiles included Donati and also Dante's trusted friend and confidant, the aged Guido Cavalcanti, who was hot-headed and argumentative. Vieri DeCerchi, the hero of Campaldino, was spared exile.

Dante went along with the exile of his friend, although it pained him greatly to do so. But in Italy any man who places principle above personal power through friendship and alliance is going against the culture. Though noble, this trait would lead to the downfall of Dante. He incurred animosity in both factions.

The sentences against the Whites and Blacks specified they must retire to certain other cities. Donati immediately ignored the terms of banishment and fled to Rome and his patron, Pope Boniface. Cavalcanti was sent to Sarzana, on the coast northwest of Florence where he contracted malaria.

The Whites decided to send a mission to the pope, requesting that the decree of excommunication against the city be lifted. Dante was part of this diplomatic party. What he saw shaped the rest of his life.

Rome

Rome, the Eternal City. *Roma, non basta una vita,* one life is not enough. My first hurried visits to the capital of Italy were in the late 1980s, and I couldn't quite get a grip on the city. Unusual for me, as I typically orient myself quickly when traveling. I visited twice, once on a health inspection, the second time when my air base was found to have extremely high levels of radon gas, and I met with Italian health officials.

I had a small hotel room near the U.S. Embassy, just off the Via Veneto. Some years earlier this fancy boulevard had been the upscale heart of Rome where diplomats, cinema stars and the idle rich found some sense of purpose in life promenading up and down the pavements, passing chic cafes occupied by similar non-occupied souls. Now the glory had faded.

I took a city tour to get my bearings, but everything seemed a great hodgepodge of churches, paintings, sculptures and overlapping, disjointed stories. Then I realized, … that is the secret of Rome. This great city is a marvelous chalkboard of history. Every street, every monument, every building has been written upon, erased, then written over again and again with the lives and stories of the Roman race. Most churches are blends of different architectural styles. It is difficult to call any building purely Renaissance, Gothic or Baroque. Most are works in progress, slowly finished over many years, sometimes centuries.

The constant is the people, more consistent, more enduring that any political program, current fad or foreign influence. They are the time machine. Romans are best understood by watching their hands. These people are famous for their gestures while talking. Hands point and stab violently when angry, move gently and tenderly when talking about love, and with palms open and fingers gently curved, follow their eyes skyward when contemplating beauty. Like everywhere else, the hands are naturally involved in eating. The difference is that eating in Rome is not consumption, it is life itself. When you dine with a Roman you share intimacy, the most sacred, common and personal part of life.

Romans touch one another constantly, in the most natural and intimate ways. In friendship, in communication, in affection. It is as natural as talking. I've watched middle-aged couples practically fondling one another as they walked down the street. Wait a minute! Forget "practically." They were fondling one another! This is one sensual city.

Priests generally keep their hands clasped behind their backs as they stroll along looking at the ground, talking seriously with one of their other clerical buddies. Strange that these supposedly spiritual gents tend to look down rather than up; I was always taught that heavenly matters were upward. Perhaps one hand grabbing another keeps both of them under control so that they don't naturally wander to anger, sex, overeating, drinking or some other wonderful pleasure.

While priests look down, the tourists are generally looking up with mouths softly open. Gazing at street signs, restaurant names, and soaring monuments.

By and large, ordinary Romans look straight ahead … meeting life head-on. Their intense eyes lock onto yours, immediately greeting you, taking your measure.

On a return pleasure trip I decided to get a better grip on the city than through one of my hurried one or two-night business trips, so my wife and I booked a reservation at a small, privately owned hotel in the center of the city, midway between the familiar Spanish Steps and the Piazza Navona. The location was perfect. When our taxi dropped us off, we were greeted by a short, round fellow who acted as a sort of doorman/greeter for the several small hotels/pensions that occupied different floors of the large building. I never figured out exactly who employed him or what his job really was, but he was an endearing fellow with one of those warm, engaging faces that seem standard issue on happy, aging Italian men. Soon my wife made friends with him (which wasn't difficult), and that meant I was automatically considered a good guy by association with her.

The entrance he attended consisted of two huge wooden doors secured by an electric lock on the inside. When both doors swung open, an ancient chariot with its driver could have roared through and it would have looked entirely appropriate. Outward appearances must mean a lot in this city because the entrance was the only part of the hotel that by itself was large. We passed through a tiny interior courtyard, climbed a narrow set of marble stairs to a minuscule elevator that lifted us two more floors to the hotel entrance. The reception area was small with one desk. Behind it sat a young gentleman who checked us in. The adjoining breakfast nook was tiny.

We had one of the best rooms in the hotel with fine antique-looking furniture. Two single beds were rammed together with just enough space on either side to shuffle sideways to your reclining spot. The bath was green swirling marble and white porcelain, and there was just enough room for me to spin around and address whichever fixture I happened to need at the moment. I'm an engineer, and I don't believe I could have done a better job of economizing space if I had worked it out for a long time.

That evening I left my room for an evening stroll. My wife was a few minutes ahead of me and as I walked across the courtyard to the massive doors, she was chatting with our doorman. Being a fine representative of the female side of the species, she was receiving his earnest, devoted, undying attention. Yes indeed, this guy was Italian. As I approached, he glanced toward me, gave a warm greeting, and as my wife and I started down the sidewalk I heard, *"Signor!"* Our new friend was pointing at the bulge in my rear pants pocket. Oh yes, the pickpockets!

"Grazie tanto, signor," I replied as I quickly switched the wallet to the front pocket. He gave me an approving smile.

Heading west we crossed the Via del Corso, the main boulevard that runs north and south right through the heart of Rome, and we aimed straight for Piazza Navona.

As we entered the piazza, I was struck with how open, airy and pleasant it was in early evening. It is shaped in a long oval that gives the immediate impression of a perfect site for ancient chariot races, which is exactly what it was. The first century emperor Domitian built his stadium here, and although he was a disastrous emperor, which was common, he was devoted to the arts and athletic contests. He revived a sort of Olympics, which took place every four years.

Tonight the center of the piazza was filled with African panhandlers and local street performers while the edges were ringed with nice restaurants and bars. Like ancient chariot drivers we circled the runway of the piazza with restaurants and their maitre d's on the perimeter, vendors and performers (mostly mimes) occupying the slightly raised inner oval. Individuals from both groups vied for our attention.

Immediately before us was one of the mimes. He was dressed as a young businessman in a fine suit, frozen mid-stride, one arm flung ahead, the trailing hand clutching a briefcase. His clothing and hair perfectly formed to give the appearance of a breeze rippling past his body. His tie flailed outward, bent back for the illusion of speed, and like all else in this picture, absolutely still. His frozen smile and unblinking eyes were dazzling. He had my vote for best performance of the evening.

Strange that you call this a performance, but that is exactly what it is, requiring strong physical and mental discipline to remain locked in position for long periods of time. Our young performer took us back in time to ancient Greek and Roman theatre where mimes performed. When the Romans adopted this art form from the Greeks, they added comic elements, and all the mimes in the piazza tonight were amusing, displaying themselves in stone-cold silence. When they did move, it was unexpected and likewise, humorous. How fascinating that in a modern world filled with so much action and frenzy, people acting like statues are so absorbing.

As with many other things, when Italians adopted the mime art form from the Greeks it was developed and enriched further, and it found a nurturing, enduring home in the hearts and lives of the deeply theatrical Italians. This country is filled with great actors, and often the best ones never reach the stage or cinema. Thousands of years after ancient Rome, finding these performers still at work makes the Piazza Navona one more time machine.

The African peddlers were on display too. Lined up on the inner oval, they sold the standard souvenirs and trinkets. Tourists passed from vendor to vendor, looking for the eternal bargain. Occasionally the line of merchants was interrupted by a solo musician, who performed facing one of the restaurants.

Vasso and I did our analysis of the restaurants by checking the menus displayed on pedestals in front of the outdoor tables. We chose one named "Tre Scalini." It looked good, and most importantly, an outside table came available while we were deciding, so we snagged it. I was anxious to try the local Frascati wine. The meal was expectedly good. After all, this was Italy. With her almost unerring sense for quality, my wife ordered divino tartufo, a swirled chocolate gelato, for dessert. It was as wonderful as it sounded. Later on we discovered this restaurant was renowned for that particular treat.

To our left a young French woman dressed elegantly in white carved out a place among the vendors and seated herself with microphone and guitar. She sang flowing love songs that sound better in French than any other language in the world.

Suddenly, all the African merchants began to move at once, quickly gathering their wares, some with cell phones to their ears, murmuring and walking briskly in the same direction like a bunch of black pigeons flapping away from the piazza in unison. The restaurant patrons glanced at one other, wondering what sudden disturbance sent the flock into flight.

Vasso flagged down the waiter. He smiled, "The police are coming. None of the vendors have permits." Just a few cell phones and the result was like telepathy.

The next morning was our time to visit the Vatican. We decided to take a "canned tour" rather than do it on our own. This way we avoided the long lines of tourists waiting eternally to see the headquarters of those who talk confidently about eternity.

Armed with our vouchers, a minivan picked us up at the hotel entrance and whisked us to Piazza Barberini, where we stood on the corner with other confused sightseers waiting for the tour to begin. Soon our herd began to move across the street toward a harmless looking bus. We followed, ignorant and wondering. At the door of the bus confusion reigned. Italians who seemed to be in charge talked about details, exchanged paperwork, seemingly oblivious to the clueless patrons of the tour. We filed on, asking each other if we were in the right place because we lacked the precise confidence to which Americans are accustomed. A short, thin Italian woman who seemed to be the guide spent an inordinate amount of time with one tourist who needed a great deal of reassurance, and who finally filed off the bus with her paperwork, going who knows where. Finally the driver appeared from nowhere, climbed into his seat and fired up the engine. As the bus began to move the tour guide turned and for the first time, spoke in English into her microphone. Within ten seconds we knew we were in the right place. I guess it is all a matter of faith.

Angela was our guide. She was Sicilian and had been doing this for twenty years. She was precise, humorous and efficient. We disembarked from the bus beside a high wall that bordered the Vatican. Angela gave each of us a radio with neck strap and an earpiece so that every person constantly heard her voice. She marched ahead holding an upright car antenna with a red handkerchief tied to the top so that we didn't lose her. We saw other tour groups; each guide had a similar antenna with a gaily colored cloth as standard equipment.

The Vatican museums are a treasure trove of great art. Angela guided us through, giving her own slant on many of the objects. Typically Italian, she was cheerful, cynical and independent. We liked her.

The highlight of any of these Vatican tours is always the Sistine Chapel. We all know of Michelangelo Buonarroti's gifted, heroic ordeal in painting the ceiling while battling with Pope Julius II over money, design, working conditions and time constraints. The sculptor who did not want to paint and yet is more famous for this ceiling than any sculpture he ever produced.

Despite the murmuring crowd and dim lighting this small chapel always awes its visitors. I was familiar with most of the panels, but in her provocative way Angela pointed out one of God, floating toward us in flowing purple robes, then an identical figure drifting away dressed the same. The retreating person's robe was parted, revealing his bare backside. Leave it to Michelangelo to provide such an image: earthy, provocative, irreverent, controversial, but above all, independent. Yes, good old Buonarroti was Italian through and through.

When the museum tour finished we loaded on the bus for our next-to-last stop, a Vatican souvenir shop. We spent much more time than needed inside the store, looking at vastly overpriced mementos, some blessed by the pope for an additional price. Angela chatted with the store employees and I wondered about possible financial strings between the souvenir shop and the tour company.

The last, optional part of the tour was a visit on our own to St. Peter's Basilica, the greatest church in Christendom. It does not disappoint. It is just as grand in real life as all the images we have seen. From the outside the Michelangelo dome and enormous church nave open into the great square bordered by straight columned porches on each side, extending to sweeping semi-circles enclosing the remainder of the square. Aerial photos give this architectural expanse the effect of head (dome), body (nave) and outstretched arms (columned porches) of a benevolent father, which is what I suppose the church is meant to represent. Inside the basilica itself is like any beautiful church but magnified without distortion to a grand scale befitting the headquarters of the worldwide Catholic Church. Walking through you get the distinct impression that God is big.

As we left the basilica we ran into our friend, Alessandro and his lovely British wife. Alex was from Milan, semi-retired, and was running as an MP (Member of Parliament) for the Northern League, a strong political party that seems to be constantly threatening separatism. Like many Italians his passions and allegiances ran deep for his region of the country. To this day, the independent provincialism of different segments of the Italian peninsula remains strong.

My wife and I grabbed a cab back to our hotel. On Alex's recommendation we dined at a small restaurant near the Piazza Parlamento. True to its name the Piazza holds the grand Italian Parliament building, glowing in the sunshine and dominating the square.

Down a narrow, shaded alleyway off the piazza we found the Restaurant da Gino. The food was delicious, the table wine came from Gino's vineyard, and I felt I was eating where the Romans eat. Since the restaurant holds only about thirty seats reservations are a good idea, otherwise you may stand waiting for a while. The pasta is homemade, thick and yellow, the vegetables are fresh and unusual dishes like rabbit pop up on the menu from day to day. With innate dignity Gino moved from table to table, ensuring that his patrons were satisfied. His waiters buzzed around with high energy and elastic faces evoking wide ranges in facial expression. Their performances were like scenes from a Roberto Benigni movie.

Gino glanced occasionally at the door, obviously on the lookout for someone. I noticed a "reserved" sign on a small table with one chair beside the cash register near the entrance. Soon a trim, handsome, well-dressed man entered, took the seat, ordered his meal, then chatted comfortably with Gino, his daughter who commanded the cash register and the waiters. But this guy was getting a little bit of special attention, and I realized he was an MP. To the right of his table on the wall hung a picture of King Juan Carlos of Spain who paid Gino's restaurant a visit once upon a time. I always suspected that Spaniard was a democrat.

We returned to the hotel and after a short nap Vasso and I headed north on the Corso. We turned right on the Via Condotti. Everyone who visits Rome has to do this. Stroll up the most fashionable street in the city to the well-known Spanish Steps. All the exclusive stores line this street, and it is a delight to read the names, look at the beautiful merchandise, then glance at the frightening prices. The street is blessedly blocked to auto traffic except for the occasional police car. As in all countries law enforcement folks do not obey every law.

The Via Condotti slanted upward. In the distance the dazzling Spanish Steps continued to rise in an increasing upward thrust crowned by Trinita dei Monti, a French church. The long promenade seemed a stairway to the sky. And isn't that just so Roman. An elegant Italian street flowing into a "Spanish" square, leading up to a church built by a king of France. That ancient ability of Italians to accept foreign elements without altering their own culture … remains. Time machine.

In a similar way we saw this enduring fusion on the streets. Romans mixed easily with tourists. The locals slid around foreigners as if both were well oiled. I looked twice at individuals or groups to guess their origins, and in most cities around the world I don't have to do that. There is something about that welcoming nature of the Romans that is apparent even in street mingling. This is the only foreign city I have ever visited where I waited to hear the words coming out of people's mouths before I decided for sure whether they were citizens.

Like an ancient amphitheater where the audience enjoys good entertainment, the Spanish steps are the traditional seats for tourists to enjoy the spectacle of Rome before them. Here they sit in sun-drenched contentment, looking down at the Piazza di Spagna with its gurgling fountain and swirling crowds. The Via Condotti stretches west into the sunset toward the Tiber River with the Vatican silhouetted beyond. The tourists all hold their admissions ticket: the standard, wonderful ice cream cone. This doesn't change.

In comparison to the expansive Piazza di Spagna, a few blocks south lies the "hemmed in" *Fontana di Trevi,* the Trevi Fountain. Made famous by several mid-twentieth century films, the fountain completely fills its square, and on most summer evenings it's "standing room only" unless you are willing to wait a bit for a seat. Because the buildings push in on all sides of the square, the delightful Roman breezes struggle to penetrate, and the heat puts a perspiring shine on the flushed, happy faces of the tourists.

Occasionally the heat pushes someone over the edge, … literally. Some years ago a Milanese woman shed all her clothes and plunged into the water. It is illegal to swim in the fountain, doubly so in the nude. She said, "I was hot. The water belongs to everyone." She was taken temporarily into police custody, but photos of the frolicking female soon splashed across the Italian news services. Unfortunately I was two months late for the show.

Luckily the ever-present spectacle of the sculptures adorning the fountain is also delightful. Neptune takes center stage, taming the waters, if not every tourist. Two goddesses are framed in the façade behind him while he stands on a seashell chariot, pulled by two horses handled by tritons. Like our risqué human bather, the half-submerged tritons are unclothed. I guess if you're mythological, it's okay.

The Trevi Fountain and the Spanish steps are fine examples of Baroque architecture, the style that followed the Renaissance. After the precision, logic and orderly beauty of the Renaissance the Italians were ready for a change, and the Baroque fuses art and architecture together. We see that in the Trevi. Rococo is an extreme form of Baroque with an abundance of adornments. These are styles that model the Italian love of all that is theatrical, and the Baroque period was one of great innovation and creativity in art. And the art was pure entertainment. Prime example ... opera.

In the 1500s, a group of men in Florence worked to revive the ancient form of Greek tragedies. They sought to put this in a musical form, but no one knew how or if the Greeks had sung their performances. This didn't stop those creative Italians. They imagined it. And thus was born the enduring spectacle of opera, with all of its drama, frills and musical beauty.

A legend has evolved based on the movie, "Three Coins in a Fountain" that says if you throw one coin in the Trevi Fountain, you will return to Rome. If you throw a second coin, you will marry in the city. And finally, if you toss in a third, you will divorce here. So budget accordingly, depending upon where you are in life, what you want to do and where you want to do it.

The next morning we walked south on the Corso. Before us in the distance was the monument to Vittorio Emanuele II, first king of modern Italy. At the epicenter of Rome's traffic swirl it towers before the Piazza Venezia like a ... well, that is the question. Some say it is a great structure, while many Italians chuckle and give it nicknames like "wedding cake," "false teeth" or "typewriter." One thing is certain. No one can ignore it.

Made of dazzling white marble, sixteen Corinthian columns curve to form the back of what to me is a grand throne with two magnificent Greek temples forming the outside edges. The seat of this great "chair" is a huge porch on which is centered a bronze equestrian statue of Victor Emanuele. There are other embellishments: fountains, statues and so on. For me the monument is a huge throne presiding over modern Italy, the resting place of the reigning spirit of a finally united Italian peninsula.

Just before the monument we turned right onto a similarly named street, the Corso Vittorio Emanuele and made our way toward Campo di Fiori, the city's great open-air fruit and vegetable market. After several blocks we turned left and wandered through cobblestone streets that led to the market. My wife worked her way through the stalls, inspecting the vegetables and fruits with the dedicated eye of a good cook and a fine merchant. She quickly fell into the very personal, Mediterranean bargaining that is an essential part of her Greek nature. On my part, I looked around and did my own assessment of the various cafes lining the square. My priorities were simple. Number one, it was very warm, so shade was paramount. Two, which of the establishments had the best breeze? Lastly, was an outside table available?

The wind was blowing generally from the west, across the Tiber and funneling down one of the side streets into the square. One of the cafes on that breezy byway was fairly full and completely shaded. A table came free and I sat down and signaled my wife. She arrived with several bags of fruit and a small coffee machine that must have been a good bargain. We'd both done our part.

In many ways, Italian cities are simply gross enlargements of villages. Although Rome has well over two and a half million inhabitants, like any smaller town, it has one, main, prominent central vegetable market. I noticed that our hotel clerks and even the owners of restaurants bragged that they bought their vegetables fresh from Campo di Fiori. In a similar way, Barzini says that the Via Veneto is like the main street in any small Italian town, just on a grander scale. It seems like you can take the Italian out of the country, but you can't take the country out of the Italian.

Tonight was opera night for us. We walked north from the Spanish Steps along the Via del Babuino, looking for the church where the performance was held. It was marked by a buzzing crowd waiting for entrance. We handed our tickets to a young lady seated behind a small desk in the foyer, then proceeded down a narrow, darkened hallway toward the center of the church. It was gloomy with rows of simple chairs lined up in the open nave. Luckily we were early so we grabbed seats near the altar, which had been converted for use as a stage.

The opera was *"La Traviata,"* the extremely popular tale of a French courtesan who falls in love, abandons her profession, falls ill, then leaves her lover because she has brought disgrace on his family, making the excuse that she wishes to resume her former life. Her lover is angry, insults her, then discovers her real motivation. They are reconciled and she dies in his arms.

This performance was so gripping and worked so well for me (although I am not an opera fan) simply because of the intimacy of the setting. We were close, practically on stage with the singers, and there was no artificial amplification of the music and singing. At the Parisian parties, at the country villa where the lovers live, we were "in" these settings with the artists who acted quite naturally in realistic clothing, not overblown gowns and tuxedos. Also the singing was quite good, but it was real communication between the cast members, not strident performances blasted at the audience from a faraway stage. Finally, the actors looked like any people you pass on the streets of Rome, which was exactly what they were.

The next morning was Sunday, and I headed out alone for the great Porta Portese flea market. For once in this wonderful "walking town" I flagged down a taxi that zipped me along the river then across one of the many small bridges to the elaborate "porta," an ancient gate that marks the entrance to the market. It's hilarious because the ornate entranceway ushers you from the open air to … the open air! But the market itself is certainly not just a façade. The largest open-air merchandise free-for-all in Europe, it is well over one hundred meters long in a straight line, crammed with booths and goods. I wound my way down the long path through throngs of customers, merchants and food vendors who were as diverse and colorful as the items for sale. Arms flying, voices shooting out, colorful shirts, skirts and tablecloths flapping like flags in the arms of sellers as they enticed and bargained with patrons.

It was blazing hot, and I couldn't exhaust the place. It did me in. I'm sure if I continued I would come upon some item that I could acquire nowhere else, but whether I could spend my money wisely was a huge question. You really haven't bargained until you've dealt with one of these characters.

I walked back through the *"porta,"* turned right and crossed the street to the bridge, hoping for some relief from the heat. The Tiber, green and polluted, oozed by beneath me, offering the slightest bit of cooling effect, but it wasn't enough. I flagged another taxi and jumped in, beating a hasty retreat to my air-conditioned hotel room.

It is impossible to say that any particular part of Rome is the overall center, the essence, the heart of the city. However, any one person can say that "For me, this is the essence of Rome." And my personal choice is the Pantheon.

For those who have not visited Rome and even for many who have, this great monument remains unknown or at least under appreciated. Located at the geographical center of the city the Pantheon lives up to its name, "All the gods." Originally built by Marcus Agrippa in 27 B.C., it was remodeled by Hadrian in the second century A.D. and converted to a Christian church by one of the popes in the 600s. Well, let's say it was "almost converted."

Unfortunately, my wife had twisted her back so I was on my own this evening. I sat at the "Bar Pantheon" just alongside the great monument, looking west as the sun set and said good night to the city once again. I ordered a pizza and a glass of red wine. At the Piazza Navona I watched and worshipped the current, vital people of Rome. In this square I sat and worshipped the enduring history of one of the greatest cities in the world. The sun set as it always has, but life went on.

The entrance to the Pantheon is a great porch of massive Corinthian columns, and the edifice itself is a giant bricked sphere with the greatest dome in the world, all the more marvelous because it is a legacy of ancient Rome, the only building to survive intact. That alone would be a miracle, but there's more.

Passing through the entrance you enter an enduring world: ancient, modern, pagan, Christian, but essentially spiritual. Once used to allow the smoke of burning pagan sacrifices to escape, the original opening at the top of the dome remains. The Pantheon contains the tombs of Raphael, Kings Victor Emmanuel and Umberto, but no churchly "saints." The resting places of the modern kings are attended by a medley of male and female uniformed officials, young and older, contentedly looking straight ahead, as diverse as any such group could be, yet very professional. The beautiful, sloped marble floor allows the raindrops that pour in through the hole in the dome to run off to drains.

Because it is spherical, not built in the shape of a cross, because of the pagan opening at the top leaving it open to all the elements of weather, and because of a thousand other ancient reasons impossible to comprehend, this temple remains a timeless step back, echoing the enduring culture that is forever Rome. I could almost see and smell the smoke rising up from the ancient animal sacrifices, lifting a prayer to "all the gods."

On our last evening in the eternal city, we walked south on the Corso toward my "giant white throne." We passed to the right of the Vittorio Emanuele monument and climbed the steps to the Piazza del Campidoglio. Here we met a group of American educators, very happy to visit Rome as part of their university jobs in international studies. Looking west the sun set on modern Rome with all its vibrancy. Car horns honking, traffic flowing in all directions. We turned around and headed east to say goodbye to "ancient Rome." We came to the grand overlook for the Roman Forum with its half-standing, half-littered marble columns deserted in the fading light. On the far side rises the Coliseum where those ancient professional athletes, the gladiators, gave thrills and amusement to the spectators. Now all was still, and for a moment, standing before two thousand years of fascinating history, between the bustling modern city and the ruins of antiquity, you could sense the spirits of the Romans mingling among the marbles. My time machine hovered between two worlds that are really one.

Back at the hotel it was time to settle the bill before our taxi whisked us to the airport in the morning. Four different, handsome young men along with the hotel owner, have been our helpers during this visit. Each one was charming in his unique and special way. Tonight Andrea was on duty, and we sat and chatted with him about the beauty of the city. It was apparent that Rome was Andrea's lover. He spoke of her sincerely and passionately, without pretense or exaggeration but with deep conviction.

"I was born here," he said, "and I doubt I will ever leave."

My wife said, "Well, the city is beautiful, and we have the popes to thank for that."

He smiled slightly. "I'm sure they realized, like everyone does, what beauty was before them."

He talked to us of the cooling breezes, the best times to visit, the prices, how some patrons return again and again. But he didn't speak of specific monuments or attractions, particular churches or piazzas. He talked holistically, not about the individual beauty spots of his mistress, but about her seamless spirit, her total attraction. He was totally devoted. He was in love with Rome.

*****

Dante and his two companions entered a Rome that in 1300 was bursting with life. Boniface had declared a "Year of Jubilee," and it was an overwhelming success. Hundreds of thousands of pilgrims had overflowed the city, bringing all the ancillary benefits of pilgrimages to Rome. It was said by one historian that "the priests used rakes to gather the money from the ground."

Boniface received the three Florentines respectfully. He had been thoroughly briefed by his ally, Donati. Dante spoke little as he was the junior member of the delegation, but Boniface carefully took in the young man before him. The plea to remove the edict of excommunication from the city of Florence was delivered, and Boniface benignly told the envoys to leave all to his paternal wisdom. Their plea was ignored.

Dante journeyed back to Florence, reassured that the remarkable city of Rome was indeed the spiritual center of the universe.

The winter of 1300-1301 passed with great uncertainty. The Blacks generally ignored their sentences and had not remained in the designated places of exile. In view of this and the pope ignoring their plea to lift the ban on Florence, her rulers decided to recall the banished Whites from their places of exile. This somewhat strengthened the city.

In the late summer of 1301 the news broke that a French prince, Charles Valois had crossed the Alps with an army and was advancing on Florence. The city flew into a frenzy.

As the exiled Blacks streamed to join the French forces, Dante rose to the moment. He assembled the leaders and prominent citizens. It was unanimously decided that another delegation go to Rome. Dante was elected as the leader.

Dante and two other envoys rushed to Rome for another audience with the pope. Again, Boniface received them with respect and again assured them that all would work out. Indeed, all had already been worked out.

In September 1301, Boniface had conferred on Charles Valois the title, "Pacifier of Tuscany." The pope "awarded" him two hundred thousand florins for his services.

The pope detained Dante in Rome and dispatched the other two envoys back to Florence with great assurances that all would be well. They returned, assembled the citizens of Florence and decided to send envoys to Charles Valois.

The French prince received the messengers cordially, promised to obey all laws and principles of liberty, and the envoys returned to Florence.

Charles Valois entered the city on November 1, 1301, unarmed and without his Black allies. He assured the citizens of his noble intentions, and he was granted dictatorial powers by the citizens of Florence. Within several days armed men appeared throughout the city, including Corso Donati and his followers. Burning and looting, they swept through the city. Dante's home was vandalized, his properties seized, and his wife and children fled to the home of a relative. Since Gemma was a cousin of Corso, her life was not in jeopardy, but the family was reduced to poverty.

Within a week grand Florence lay desolate, charred and smoking, as if sacked by barbarian hordes. Charles Valois journeyed to confer with the pope, and the Blacks were in control. Dante and other White leaders were charged with crimes against the city. The two charges against the Poet were resisting the authority of Charles Valois and misuse of public money. Both charges were groundless. A huge fine and two years banishment from Florence was the sentence against Dante. He was given until March 10th to pay the fine. His assets seized, it was impossible to raise the amount. Dante remained in Rome and promptly on March 11th, the final decree was issued. Dante Alighieri was eternally banished from Florence. If found in the city he would be burnt alive. Penniless and despondent, the Poet and former leader of Florence left Rome and made his way to Siena.

Siena

Siena, the beloved. The city rises majestically on a huge hill of dark orange clay and lends its name to the color "burnt sienna." Throughout history it was the rival of nearby Florence, the city-state that eventually eclipsed it.

Great walls enclose all of Siena, making it a living medieval relic, peopled by modern Italians. It is a town I could easily learn to live in and love.

Like many Italian cities, the streets meander in a labyrinth pattern that is at first disorienting. After checking into our small hotel, my wife and I wandered the streets and magnetically found the central Piazza del Campo, social heart of the city. A huge, scalloped, cobblestone gathering-place, I've never seen anything quite like it. A fan-shaped valley of smooth rocks with a wide promenade ringing the top, locals and visitors sit and recline on the sloping stones like loungers in a large city park. Cafes and restaurants ring the promenade that each year is transformed into a horse racing track for the annual "palio." Large quantities of dirt are hauled in and deposited to ready it for this very passionate horse race. Each horse represents one of the many city "clubs," and winning the race is a yearlong source of intense pride to members. The clubs are organized around various streets of the town, so really it is a horserace of competing neighborhoods.

We settled at an outdoor café table, ordered wine and appetizers. It was Sunday evening, and within a few minutes the music of a marching band erupted at the entrance of one of the eleven streets flowing into the piazza. Soon a large, organized procession of young boys marched into the square, dressed in colorful medieval garb, puffy berets and pantaloons of soft, rich colors. Parading around, they twirled huge flags with great fanfare and precision, offering us a wonderful spectacle. So often in Italy a simple glass of wine at a café buys the finest entertainment.

As the pageant ended the participants along with numerous other people filed into one of the streets branching off the piazza. Although the street looked no different than any other, on this night it was brightly lit and lined with long dinner tables, draped with white tablecloths and laden with food. It was party time for one of the neighborhood clubs.

We strolled up the street and watched the locals as they talked and laughed, comfortable with friends and neighbors they have lived a lifetime around. Food and drink were delivered to the tables with great enthusiasm and no discernible pattern. This is one of the supreme joys of travel. I felt I was not only watching an exotic foreign cinema, I was standing in the center of the movie set. To the marvelous actors all around us, my wife and I were invisible.

The next evening we walked up a different street, looking for a restaurant. We chose a humble place with four tables on a narrow sidewalk. My chair looked up a steeply ascending avenue whose streetlight fixtures were all freshly painted with vivid Tuscan colors in the same distinct pattern. Puzzled, my wife flagged down a local teenage boy as he strolled by, and she asked for an explanation.

He told us the light fittings were proudly painted this year because the neighborhood's horse won the annual palio. Deftly the young man flipped open his cell phone, clicked on the video button and handed the instrument to us. On its small screen we watched the annual horserace, complete with skilled riding, hazardous passes and scary falls by several horses and riders. Little wonder he was so proud of this year's winner.

We returned to our hotel and stopped by the reception desk to pick up the room key. The clerk listened intently as my wife spoke English with a slight accent, and he had an odd look on his face. Suddenly he responded to her in Greek. Surprised, we realized this young man who we assumed was Italian was actually from Vasso's country. An instant bonding and closeness ensued. While we talked an attractive young girl entered the reception area from the street, and we met his Greek girl friend. Andrew and Georgia were students in Siena, and we grew to know them fairly well over the next few days.

"Andrew, what should we do for breakfast tomorrow morning?"

"Well, you can have breakfast here at the hotel, but it is just as good and cheaper to simply go around the corner to the coffee bar for a brioche."

Early the next morning while my wife was still asleep, I quietly left the room, descended the staircase to the hotel's street exit and walked up the street. I turned left and a sign for one of Italy's numerous coffee brands jutted out above a door halfway down the block.

I walked into the small bar; the strong odor of coffee and the buzz of morning conversation greeted me. The girl behind the counter looked at me with a question on her face that required no greeting.

"Un cappuccino e' un brioche." I said.

"Si."

As she went to work on my order, I watched the morning's patrons and realized this walled city was not merely another tourist trap. It was a true working town. Smartly dressed businesswomen and men filtered in and out, drank their morning pick-me-ups, chatted with other customers, deposited euros near the cash register, then moved on to business.

Engaged in animated talk, two attractive young women were drinking coffee at the bar. A heavy-set man entered with a happy face, a casual sweater and an assertive look. He passed the women, ordered his coffee then engaged them in conversation. They obviously knew him well. He was both a comedian and a harmless flirt. The girls relaxed, smiled, chatted with him and finished their coffee. As they turned to go, one of the women reached up and patted him on the cheek, a nice gesture … but he didn't have a chance.

I love the way Italians are so comfortable with one another. Conversation is immediate, direct, uninhibited, seldom hesitant, unsure or clumsy. Everything is straightforward and relaxed. A businessman entered in a three-piece suit, and the local comedian resumed the same sort of conversation with him. Coffee bars are such democratic places.

Back at the hotel Andrew and Georgia told me that things were not so easy in Greece and Italy right now. There were constant complaints about that most undemocratic of government implementations, the euro. Southern Europeans (and I discovered, a great many northern Europeans) maintained that the universal currency has made life more difficult. Andrew said his brother in Greece with a master's degree earned less salary than Andrew made as a hotel clerk in Italy. Often what made financial survival possible in these countries was the security of family ties. Dowries, family assistance to widows, living with parents for long periods of early adulthood. There were many aspects of communal life that have been seldom seen in mainstream North America.

Siena has sharply ascending and descending streets and alleys. Flat stone slabs protrude from the walls of palaces and other buildings, providing benches for three or four occupants. Often these gathering spots are positioned well above the sidewalk; a step may provide access. The occupants of these benches have a bird's-eye view of passers-by. Over and over I saw several men chatting with each other on these roosts, like parakeets on a perch, chirping and looking down. Siena soars above the Tuscan countryside, and likewise its natives gaze down on the world passing by just below them.

Our last morning in Siena, we prepared to leave. Andrew worked the evening shift at the hotel last night, but he managed to awake to see us off. Siena's motto through the centuries has been, "It opens its heart to you." It opened that heart to the refugee Dante. The city has opened its heart to Greek students Georgia and Andrew. Bleary-eyed and unshaven, he waved an openhearted good-bye to us.

I want to return.

*****

Dante Alighieri trudged up the road to the city of Siena, head down, dark orange dust swirling around his feet. He was alone, … very alone.

I do my best to envision what Dante's life could have been like. At this point it is difficult to imagine. He was a man of great talents, some nearly unsurpassed. He was scrupulously honest and had a clear opinion of his own intelligence and abilities. No one could accuse him of being falsely humble. Vain, yes. Prone to melancholy, certainly. Brilliant, persuasive, but he had made a fatal error, and because of circumstances that error marred the rest of his life. In the swirling politics of Italy, he had placed "the commune, Florence, above all!" A noble position, but a naïve one for a politician.

His life can be viewed in three major stages. From birth to about thirty years, he was coming of age. Growing up, gaining an education, discovering his talents and desires, acquiring skills, what all of us do as our lives play out. Phase two was thirty to maybe forty years of age, his life devoted to politics. As many highly skilled individuals, he was drawn to the allure of public life, encouraged by family and friends to do what so many of us deem important.

Although deeply disillusioned he is still in this political season of his life. Later on he will move to the next phase, but that lies a few years ahead.

He settled in with members of the White party in Siena and waited for news from home. The Whites of Florence had been routed and fled the city. Some arrived in Siena, and the news they carried was not good. The Black party was firmly entrenched, giving vent to all the anger built up when they were banished. Chief among them was Corso Donati, whose rage was barely controlled.

Now we begin to see the theme so common and recurrent in Italian politics. The White Guelphs, supposedly a party of the church, began to form an alliance with the Ghibellines, the party of the emperor. With the Black Guelphs supported by the pope now in control of Florence, true to Italian political nature, factions began to ally to counterbalance the strength of their opponents in power. One can only imagine the hushed conversations in coffee shops and wine bars, eyes darting quickly, hands shielding mouths, leaning toward companions in confidence. The stuff idle men do to feel important. This has scarcely changed even to the current day. Today our clothing looks different, and we have cell phones.

Dante had little patience with false appearances, and he began to wander through Tuscany, keeping an eye on developments in Florence, visiting other White leaders. His conviction grew that the only answer would be a "universal monarch," someone who could counterbalance the power of the church. This monarch's authority must lie in temporal affairs, while the church would properly remain in the sphere of spiritual matters. Alighieri believed absolutely in his God and his church. Just as fervently he believed that Rome should be the political capital of his world. The dream of Frederick II traveled on through time gaining momentum. To Frederick's powerful sword would soon be added Dante's magnificent pen.

In 1303, Dante traveled to Verona as the guest of the ruler, Bartolommeo della Scala. A deep friendship developed, and although the Poet was restless still, he remained as the guest of della Scalla for nine months. During this time Dante cooperated with the Whites and sought to gain support for a move against the Blacks. Several ill-fated and disastrous attempts were made to retake Florence, but they ended in defeat. Dante became more and more frustrated with the failures of the Whites to cooperate, plan and align themselves with the Ghibellines successfully.

Verona

Every year on the 13th of December, the Santa Lucia market is held in the central area of Verona. When we lived in Italy, since our oldest son's birthday was the same day, we made it a family habit to visit Verona on that date. The ancient centers of Italian towns are generally constructed of stone, and Verona is no exception. A fine, well preserved Roman arena stands in the center of town and dominates life, summer and winter.

The stones are cool in summer and very cold in winter. The winter market is a lively affair, booths full of holiday trinkets and food, shaggy-faced merchants dressed in equally shaggy coats drinking heated wine and blowing steam from their mouths onto their hands, keeping their palms ready to change merchandise for money.

We walked toward the arena, entered and made our way around the interior passage. Since Christmas was nearly upon us miniature nativity sets were displayed one after another in niches of the wall. The Christmas scenes were from different countries, and in this very representative Italian town we saw a worldwide display of different cultures' renditions of the Christmas scene: Madonna, newborn child, father, angels, shepherds and wise men. Each culture saw the scene in its own eyes with its own characteristic costumes, facial features and background vegetation. Therefore each scene was different, but the theme was the same.

There was no warm spot to stand, and if you remained still the cold traveled up through your heels and leg bones to the rest of your body. The only way to forget and avoid the chill was to keep moving.

My wife and I returned in summer for an opera in the same arena. We sat in the nearby piazza in early evening and imitated the rest of the crowd by ordering a pizza and beer before the evening's performance of "Aida." The food, drink and heat made me very thirsty so like all the others I purchased a liter of bottled water and carried it into the arena. We found our place on the stone seats as the sun set, and the opera's first act began.

I didn't know much about opera at this point in my life so Vasso outlined the story. Horses and soldiers, tombs and tragedy, all very dramatically portrayed. The woman who had the title role sang her part with great passion, emotion climbing to what seemed like a climax. She sang a note then paused, and from the top of the arena a young male voice in the cheap student seats shouted with great conviction, "Shame!"

I was shocked. The audience had been listening in respectful silence so I whispered to my wife, "What was that?"

"It was a very high note, and she changed it. Must not have been able to reach it."

Amazing. How seriously these people take their artistic expression and accomplishments. And doubly surprising that a young student would know the notes so well and have the passion and confidence to express his displeasure. That's Italy.

*****

While Dante wandered about Tuscany his old nemesis, Pope Boniface was having his own share of problems. Just as he had strongly interfered in Florentine politics, Boniface continued on many other fronts and pushed papal authority to the extreme of its historical limits. He came into serious conflict with Phillip IV, King of France. As so often occurs the struggle was over power and money. Phillip blocked French church money from going to Rome, and in the autumn of 1303 he sent emissaries to Boniface's retreat in Agnani, Italy.

Demands were made, Boniface declared that "he would sooner die" than give in, and he was assaulted and beaten. The pope in his late sixties, died one month later.

Dante deeply resented the actions of Boniface which had resulted in his exile, but he condemned the assault on the pope as a shameful attack upon the church. Dante's patron and friend, della Scala, also died around this time, and frustrated with the White Guelphs Alighieri declared himself "a party unto himself," broke with the Whites and left Verona.

Earlier we said that Dante's life could be divided into three stages: coming of age, the political life, and now his life as a writer really came into focus. From this point he devoted his energies to his literature, exploring new areas, ending with his greatest and lasting achievement, the Divine Comedy. In doing so he became the true master of dramatic writing.

It is telling that when the Poet made his break with the Whites and departed Verona, his first stops were Bologna and Padua. He returned to the university cities where his advanced formal education had taken place. He was traveling both philosophically and physically toward his ultimate destiny, … he became the greatest writer in Italian history.

Dante took up residence in Bologna and reconnected with his friend, the poet Cino de Pistoia. His friend was a member of the Black Guelphs, but now this was of little importance to Alighieri; he had mentally moved beyond personal political involvement. In Bologna he completed the *"Vulgar Eloquentia."* In this landmark work, he argued for the use of vernacular Italian over Latin in poetry, and he identified fourteen separate Italian dialects, a first.

Here is the emergence of Dante's democratic principles, reasoning for the use of the common language over the Latin of the learned class, bringing literacy to the average person.

Dante was penniless, and he had to scratch out a living by any means possible. Accepting the patronage of political leaders was uncertain, sometimes demeaning and an irritation to his personal pride. However his reputation as a skilled diplomat was widespread, and from time to time opportunities arose to mediate disputes.

After a short time in Padua he traveled to Carrara in western Tuscany, near the coast and site of the famous marble quarries. Here he served as diplomat for the local ruler. During this time Dante completed *"Convivio,"* his celebration of lyric poetry.

From 1307 to 1310, Dante truly wandered. In fact there is no sure record of his whereabouts. The strongest belief is that he actually left Italy, crossed the Alps and spent time in Paris.

Paris

I first visited Paris in the late 1970s. Vasso and I rolled into town on the overnight train from Salzburg, Austria (the famed Orient Express). A young German man shared our compartment, and he was effusive about Paris.

"You know, they have a McDonald's in Paris now."

"Really," I replied. "I think I'll pass on that attraction."

"No, no, you really should go. It is right on the Champs Elysees."

"Right."

As we climbed off the train, it was hissing loudly like trains always do when stopping. But I heard a different type of hissing sound in the background. It came from a nearby café. Steam spouting from a cappuccino maker. A nice, familiar greeting at seven in the morning.

We found our hotel on the Left Bank near the Latin Quarter. The manager was a young man named Claude, and he had as much character as the hotel. Young, frizzy-haired, he circulated in pajamas and slippers and was obsessed with playing old vinyl records of classical music. Occasionally, when distracted, he somewhat managed the hotel. Over the next few days, we became acquainted with Claude's father who was a Polish refugee, having fled from behind the Iron Curtain just after World War II by hiding in the bowels of a coal freighter that docked in France.

This is what I loved about Europe as a young man, running into real characters with stories as interesting as their appearances. Paris abounded in them.

I had been eagerly reading my guidebooks and had a desire to try Algerian couscous, probably because the name sounded exotic. That evening we asked Claude about a restaurant that I had heard about that featured this dish.

"Oh, you needn't go that far. Outside our hotel, just go right, then turn left down the first alley. Thirty meters on the left you will see a light. Just go right in. They serve fine couscous."

So we did. I can't say the doorway of the alleyway establishment filled me with confidence, but we plunged in anyway.

I was transported to an old black and white movie set. There were no other colors in view. A single bare light bulb hung over a dark bar. The barman was stout, middle-aged, with a white apron, slicked down black hair, and a pencil-thin, handlebar mustache coated in wax. His eyebrows directed us to a nearby table draped in white, and soon we were enjoying the North African delicacy with a nice French table wine. The meal was ample reward for being extras in this movie set.

Over the next few days we wandered Paris. Bookstores in the Latin Quarter, the Louvre (where we completely overdosed on great art), Notre Dame cathedral, apple tarts at the top of the Eiffel Tower, and the mid-morning, hung-over seediness around Montmartre and the Pigalle nightclub area.

And I hate to admit it, but I yielded to the temptation and paid a visit to the Paris McDonald's. No new experience there, but I knew I was in the American franchise that was taking over the world. After our meal, there was a greater volume of paper wrappers piled on the table than the amount of food we had consumed.

One Sunday morning we strolled in the crisp, cold air and brilliant sunshine near the Eiffel Tower. As we were about to step off the curb a late model BMW roared to a stop near us and a swarthy looking character jumped out and accosted us in broken English. He ushered us to the trunk of his auto, popped open the lid, and there lay a stack of new leather coats.

"Here, my friend, try one on."

"No, I don't think so," I replied as I grabbed Vasso's arm and began to move away.

"No! Wait, wait! They are very nice, brand new, for free!"

When I heard that, my resolve and grip on her arm began to tighten as I shook my head.

"You don't understand, Signor. Here, look!" He pulled a passport from his coat pocket, opened it and held it for me to read. An Italian passport with the man's likeness staring out at me and his birthplace listed as Naples.

That did it. I had no clue what this fellow's scheme was, but mine was a sharp exit strategy.

I looked into his face, smiled and said, "Definitely, no," then turned away from his suddenly scowling face. He jumped back in his car and sped off.

That was our 20th century visit to Paris. Years later we made an early 21st century visit, and much had changed. This time we stayed at a nice hotel located inside Charles DeGaulle airport and took the train into town. The city seemed even more crowded and the lines of tourists were daunting. So overwhelming in fact that we skipped most of the usual tourist haunts. Many more non-native French. The Latin Quarter had lost its old time quaintness, and it was just more commercial and filled with mostly middle Eastern restaurants. However there was one area we truly enjoyed strolling and that was around the Ile Saint-Louis. We left the Ile de la Cite, the island in the middle of the Seine River that proudly holds Notre Dame Cathedral, wandered over the bridge to its smaller sibling isle, and the crowds melted away. If there is a romantic spot left in central Paris, this is it. Of course there are some tourists, but hardly the mass gaggle we encountered elsewhere. Circling the edges of the island on its cobblestoned streets you can almost recapture some of that time gone by.

*****

It was now 1306 on the calendar, and ironically the papacy, which had been so instrumental in exiling Dante from his Florentine home, was itself exiled. The pope fled Rome, and the center of the Catholic Church now found a home in Avignon, France. The "Avignon exile" would last seventy years, and Dante would never again see his church headquartered in Rome.

For once, our poet wavered, wondered, and wandered. Perhaps his Florence, his Rome, his Church, his culture was not the central force in the western world. Perhaps he should look elsewhere. The Poet made his way to Genoa, boarded a freighter and headed for Marseilles in the south of France.

Marseilles was an exotic, busy port. More than any harbor in Italy, it bustled with merchants from north Africa, the Middle East, all the lands surrounding the Mediterranean and beyond. There Dante made arrangements for overland passage to Paris.

In the 1300s Paris was swelling in size and influence. A great university was growing on the Left Bank of the river Seine. Originally the Medieval University of Paris, in the late 1200s, a school of theology was founded by a church-trained man named Robert Sorbon. He was born into a poor family, but rose through the church to become the confessor of King Louis IX. The university eventually took the name of this cleric and became known as the Sorbonne. It attracted scholars like Dante from all over the known world.

He arrived in Paris and made his way to the university area in the Latin Quarter, so named because Latin was the spoken language among the educated people of the day. Ironically, Dante Alighieri, the champion of the common

Italian language, found himself mingling, conversing and studying in the formal tongue.

Meanwhile back in Italy, change continued apace. In 1308, the man who had been so instrumental in Dante's exile, Corso Donati finally pushed his ambitions and personality too far. When Donati and the forces of Charles Valois had taken Florence, even some of Corso's allies were shocked and disturbed by his vicious destruction. His ambition and arrogance were extreme. The Blacks were squabbling within their own ranks and Donati pushed his authority further and further. He took delight in ignoring laws and established procedures.

Rumors abounded that he had poisoned his first wife. His current wife was a sister of Uggucione, the conqueror of Lucca, and Donati counted on him for support. Donati hired assassins to rid himself of opponents, and his own sister had fled his presence, entering a convent and taking the vows. Undaunted, Corso scaled the convent wall, barged into the church, abducted his sister and forced her into a political marriage.

Finally, he was accused of plotting to overthrow Florence with the help of Uggucione and sentenced to exile. With a band of his followers he took refuge in his home, but his followers deserted him. He fled from the city, fighting his way out by sword.

In the countryside he was captured by mercenary soldiers who decided to return him to Florence. Rather than be delivered into bondage, he flung himself from his horse and one of the soldiers drove a lance through his face, killing him instantly.

Meanwhile, Dante completed *"De Monarchia,"* his work on the relationship of empire and papacy. And he began the work that would occupy the remainder of his life, "The Divine Comedy."

However, the restless Poet had not found the satisfaction or contentment he sought in Paris. He made his way back south across the Alps. In 1311, Henry VII of Luxembourg was crowned King of Lombardy in Milan. Dante was present at the coronation and paid homage to the young king. The Poet's hope rose that perhaps this monarch was the one to establish a healthy balance between church and state. The following year Henry was crowned Holy Roman Emperor by a cardinal in Rome (remember, the papacy had moved to Avignon). But as often happened in Dante's life, people important to him had the distressing habit of dying at inopportune times and often prematurely. Young Henry died in 1313.

From 1312 through 1318, Dante resided again in Verona as the guest of the new ruler, Can Grande della Scala. These years provided a time of stability for the Poet; the della Scala family had produced several fine rulers who formed true friendships with Alighieri. He grew very close to Can Grande, and this ruler became Dante's model of knightly manhood. The Poet finished the most famous portion of his Comedy, *"Inferno."*

Midway through his sojourn in Verona, Dante made a side trip to the city of Lucca, controlled by his friend Uggucione. He went to help a remarkable friend.

*****

A knock came at the door. Dante looked up from his writing desk. "Come."

The door opened, a palace servant entered two paces and said, "His Excellency asks for you, Signor Alighieri."

The Poet slowly placed his quill on the parchment. "Tell him I come."

"Si, Signor." He turned and departed.

Dante rose, walked to the window and splashed water on his face from the wash basin. He peeled off his robe, laid it aside and donned a vest.

Walking down the corridor, he heard occasional shuffling and muffled voices behind closed doors. Can Grande della Scala's palace was very quiet although many servants moved about throughout the building. One of the things Dante admired about his patron. Efficient, dignified, and strong. One side of the Poet's mouth turned up a bit and he thought, *"Perhaps that is why I seem to have spent more time in Verona than other places."*

The corridor widened and Dante came to the doors of the assembly hall. He spoke to the guard at the door.

"My lord has asked for me."

"You may enter, Signor."

He walked through the double doors into a large, high ceilinged room. Across the far wall was a line of windows, framed with metal bars, the borders trimmed with stained glass. A tall man gazed out the window, thumb and forefinger stroking a salt and pepper beard, hair closely cropped.

At the sound of the footsteps the tall man turned, saw Dante approaching, and smiled broadly.

"Buon giorno, Signor Dante."

"Good morning, Excellency."

"How goes your 'Burning Book'?"

Dante smiled, and his eyes twinkled. "Full of surprises."

"Perhaps I have one for you." Can Grande reached inside his maroon cloak, drew a folded parchment and handed it to the Poet. A wax seal with the imprint of a signet ring held the document together. "It arrived by courier this morning, addressed to you."

Alighieri took the letter and examined the seal. His eyes widened. Immediately he tore it open. He scanned the lines. Dante's gaze went blank for a few moments, then he looked up at della Scala.

"I must take my leave of you, Signor," he said. "Is the courier still here?"

"Yes, he waits outside," Can Grande said. "You go to Lucca?"

"Yes."

"It is dangerous. Uggucione is bringing the city under control. There is turmoil."

"Uggucione is a good friend. I will be safe."

"With him. But the roads are not safe for anyone traveling alone. I will send a squad of soldiers to escort you."

"That is kind, Excellency. Once again, I am indebted to you."

Della Scala's mouth showed a tiny smile. "And that is not easy for you."

Dante looked straight at him. "You know it is not."

"God keep you, Poet."

"Thank you, Signor. I leave within the hour."

Alighieri turned, and the lord of Verona's eyes narrowed and watched him depart.

They drove all night through a pouring rain, but by morning the rain had ceased and the dawn came with overcast skies. The carriage carrying Dante and the courier from Lucca thundered toward the city of Lucca, set like many prominent Italian hill towns on the crest of a hill. The walls of Lucca came into view on the horizon, and Alighieri leaned out of the carriage side door. Lines of smoke rose from behind the walls like gray tree trunks that branched out into dirty, white, leafy clouds. Dante settled back onto the seat and once again unfolded the parchment.

My dear friend, Signor Alighieri,

It is now some years since I last had the pleasure of your company. Those memories are as bright as yesterday's sunrise. The witty stories, the verbal swordplay, the poetry and songs, the laughter of my friends as we bantered long into the night of philosophies and histories. But most of all, how you always harmonized and knitted together the complicated plot lines of our reverie. I would that your life had such harmony.

Up until now, my life has enjoyed such, and that is the reason for my correspondence to you.

The wonderful, tranquil life has vanished in a flash. As you must be aware, Lord Uggucione has conquered our city. All of my life, my husband has been my shield and benefactor, and I learned to trust in his wisdom and providence.

Now, at our most perilous hour, my husband lies quite ill. In truth, he is dying. Our physicians have confirmed this to me.

In our world, a woman whose husband is much older comes to realize that this is her future. In my case, because my husband is well born and prosperous, I would have no anxiety when he passed from the scene.

Alas, his sickness has no hope, is a bit premature, and it comes amidst a true calamity.

Lord Uggucione's men lay waste to much of our city. Homes have been vandalized, property taken, victims have fallen without trial.

That this is too often the course of events in our times, it is no less a catastrophe. I find myself reduced to asking for your help. Something that is outside my nature, but my desperation pleads for it.

I know Lord Uggucione is your close friend. If you could intercede for our family, I would be eternally grateful. So far, our influence and friends have shielded us from harm. But some of those friends are now being attacked and their possessions seized. I foresee the same fate for my household.

If Signor Uggucione holds a fraction of the esteem that I hold for you, and which you justly deserve, I am sure that a word from you would be priceless in my behalf.

It is with a heavy yet fearful heart that I ask this, my dear Alighieri. I know of nowhere else to turn.

With undying respect and sincerity,

Signora Gentucca Morla

Dante refolded the paper and slipped it inside his cloak. Suddenly, one of della Scala's escorts pulled his horse close to the carriage and pounded his fist on door. Alighieri leaned close to the small, curtained opening above the door handle and pulled the fabric aside.

Above the roar of the wheels and horses, he shouted to the horseman. "Yes!"

The soldier bent near to the horse's neck. "Signor, we draw close. I raise a flag of peace. I suggest you prepare to speak quickly."

"I am prepared."

The horseman nodded, pulled away slightly, and the carriage began to slow. In a few moments it ground to a halt.

Dante immediately swung open the door and stepped down. The high brown walls of Lucca towered above them. Four guards stood before a large oak gate that blocked an entrance through the wall. One of them advanced. He carried a long spear, and a two-edged sword hung at his waist.

Dante took one step toward the armed man. "I am Dante Alighieri. I am a friend and ally of Lord Uggucione, and I have business with him."

"What is the nature of your business?"

Dante raised his head slightly, widened his eyes, and raised his voice a notch. "My business is with Lord Uggucione … alone."

The guard glanced at Dante's companions, noting their weapons and the crests emblazoned on their garments. "Follow me, Signor. Your escorts remain here."

Dante stood fast. "My escorts go with me."

"These men of Verona are not our allies."

"Neither are they your enemies." Dante lowered his voice but spoke clearly and slowly. "I do not believe Lord Uggucione would be pleased to know you are quibbling with his trusted friend."

The lines on the guards face softened. "Very well, Signor." He turned, walked to a nearby horse and mounted. Directing his gaze to his fellow guards, he barked, "Open the gate!"

Dante's carriage followed the mounted men through the gate and down a broad avenue. They entered a large piazza, and the horsemen pulled up and dismounted. Before them was a large stone building with columns fronting it.

The guard looked at Dante, "Follow me, Signor." Alighieri followed the guard up the marble steps and into a broad entranceway. A large open doorway looked into a high-ceilinged room.

A deep voice boomed above the buzzing conversation inside. "What in the name of God do you mean, 'Progress is slow!' I do not tolerate slow."

The guard motioned for Dante to wait in the entranceway, then turned and strode into the large room. Dante moved slightly to the right to see the occupants of the room more clearly, and a smile spread on the Poet's face.

A giant of a man stood at the end of a long table, his handsome face lined, a thick mane of white hair flowing back over his head. He pounded on the table, let out another curse, and the men around him glanced sideways and down, but did not respond.

The guard approached the giant, made a motion to speak, whispered in the big man's ear. His huge head spun toward the door, he saw Dante, and a huge smile revealed gleaming white teeth to match his hair.

He deserted the table, walked toward Alighieri.

As he neared Dante, the voice shot out, "Alighieri, you old scribe, how are you?" Grabbing the smaller man by the shoulders, he gave him a double hug and embrace, almost lifting Dante off the floor.

After a round of laughing and back slapping, the big man said, "What brings you here, my friend? Are you tired of that scoundrel, Della Scala?"

"No, matters are fine in Verona. I come to ask a favor."

The smiled vanished from Uggucione's face. "What is it?"

"I have a dear friend here in Lucca. She fears for her safety. Her husband is fairly prosperous, and he is ill."

"Where do they live?"

"Via Antonio Mordini."

The big man turned and shouted into the large room.

"Roberto! Pronto!"

A young, powerful looking man emerged from the room and walked quickly to Lord Uggucione. His face was blank.

"Si, Signor."

"Roberto, this is Signor Dante Alighieri. You know of him?"

"Of course, my Lord."

"He is my trusted ally. He has local friends who fear for their safety."

Turning to Dante, "What was the name of that street?"

"Via Antonio Mordini. It is near the amphitheater."

The younger man's eyebrows raised. "Lord Uggucione, I believe our soldiers are in that area now."

"Take men, Roberto! And Signor Alighieri. Protect his friends, leave a guard at the house. *Subito!"*

The young man looked at the Poet. "Can you ride, Signor Dante?"

"Of, course."

Roberto turned and walked quickly toward the entrance. Dante embraced his huge friend, then followed the younger man outside.

Roberto was moving toward a group of horses and men to his right. "Two men, four horses! Quickly!"

Two soldiers grabbed the reins of nearby horses, and another man led two other mounts toward Roberto. Roberto took the reins of one horse and quickly mounted. Spinning around, he barked, "Help the gentleman up!"

Soon the four men were moving quickly down the cobblestone streets, horses' hooves clicking metallically beneath them. Dante and Roberto were in the lead. Alighieri turned in his saddle.

"This is the street, Roberto! This way!"

Dante turned the horse to the right and slowed. The Via Mordini was a shambles. Furniture and clothing were scattered everywhere. Pockets of smoke swirled. Armed soldiers were yelling, throwing objects from windows. Suddenly, a woman screamed.

Roberto spoke. "Where is the house, Signor Dante?"

"Fifty meters, on the left."

"Come!"

Roberto spurred his horse, weaving through the piles of wreckage, some smoldering.

Dante halted his horse. The door of the elegant stone home was ajar. The sound of wooden objects breaking came from inside. "This is it!"

Roberto leaped from his horse, Dante and the other two soldiers close behind. The first man drew his sword, rushed through the entrance and yelled.

"Halt! In the name of Lord Uggucione!"

The noise immediately stopped, while outside the clamor continued. An older woman lay sobbing on the floor, her blouse torn open. A man dressed in simple servant's clothing was lying on the side of the room, moaning, blood on his shirt.

"Where is Signora Morla?" Dante screamed. He bent over the fallen woman but didn't touch her.

"Signora Francesca, you remember me? It is Signor Dante."

The woman looked up with terrified eyes, and a look of recognition swept over her face.

"Where is Signora Gentucca?"

A shaking finger pointed toward an ascending stairway.

The stairway led up to an open balcony. Gaping down, two soldiers stood at the rail.

One of them said, "Signor Roberto?"

Roberto nodded and ran up the steps, Dante behind him. The two soldiers met him at the head of the stairs.

Roberto spoke firmly, "Halt your operations here, this home is under the protection of Lord Uggucione."

One of the men gasped, "Signor Roberto, my God! We did not know …"

"You were doing your job," Roberto cut in.

"But Lord Uggucione will have our heads!"

"Don't worry. Where is the lady of the house?"

The man pointed toward a large oak door. "Someone is bolted inside that room. We were about to smash in."

"You are dismissed. Go downstairs and put things back in order. Then leave and continue your work. Make sure there are no fires nearby, particularly in nearby buildings. This house must be safeguarded."

"Yes, sir!"

The two men descended the stairs. Dante walked to the locked door. "Signora Morla?"

Silence.

"Signora Gentucca, it is Dante. Dante Alighieri."

Dante detected movement behind the door. A metallic snap and the door opened a crack.

"Signor Dante, is that you?"

"Yes, my dear. Open the door. You are safe."

The door opened slowly. A slim, attractive woman stood alone, a dagger clutched in her hand. A moment's pause, the dagger dropped to the floor, and the woman leaped into Dante's arms.

"Oh, Dante. You came. Thank God!"

Suddenly the woman began to sob, her breaths coming in huge gasps.

"Easy, Signora. Everything is all right. Come."

Alighieri led her to a nearby sofa, sat down with her and put his arm around her shoulder. After a few moments silence, the crying eased and Dante asked gently, "Where is your husband?"

"He is in the room."

Dante looked puzzled.

"He has been in a coma for some weeks."

Roberto had been standing silently, watching. "Signor Alighieri, my men are cleaning things up, and I shall take a look at the injured man. I will leave a guard posted outside."

"Thank you, Signor."

Roberto turned and walked toward the staircase.

The lady had begun to compose herself. The crying had ceased and she began to run her hand through her long auburn hair.

"Thank God you came when you did, Dante. I must look frightful."

"You look wonderful. You have been through quite an ordeal."

She looked up and smiled. "But we are safe now with you here. I am in your debt."

"There are no debts between friends. Tell me about your husband."

She looked away. "His health has been failing for months. The heart is weak. Then about a fortnight ago, he suddenly collapsed. He has been unconscious ever since."

"Will he recover?

"The physicians say no. But they say he is in no pain. However, he is wasting away. How long life will stay with him, I cannot guess. Would you care to see him?"

Dante nodded without desire. "All right."

She rose and led him through the bedroom door. Near the window a large canopied bed held a thin, motionless figure, submerged beneath several blankets. They drew close and Dante looked down.

Alighieri had not known the man well. He was often away on business, and his wife was at the center of Lucca's intellectuals and literary people. She was greatly respected for her intelligence and wit, and her marriage to a prosperous man had given her the freedom to pursue such a life.

He could barely recognize the man. The energy, color, and firm flesh of years ago had vanished. He was thin, white haired, skin gray with no hint of flushing. The breathing was barely perceptible.

"Gentucca, I will check how things are going downstairs. They gave your home quite an exercise."

She nodded; he turned and silently left the room.

As Dante reached the first floor he surveyed the damage. It really wasn't too bad. The original soldiers had departed to resume looting the city to replenish the coffers of Uggucione. The two soldiers who had accompanied him and Roberto remained. One was tending to the stricken man. The servant lady, Francesca sat nearby. Dante walked toward her.

She sprang to her feet, immediately kneeled, grabbed Alighieri's hand, kissing it profusely. "Oh, Signor Dante, if you had not come we were finished! Oh, thank God, thank God, thank God." Her repetitions turned to mumbling and she began to cry softly.

"But, I did come, Francesca. Are you all right?"

"Yes, I think so."

"Who is the man?"

"My husband, we are the only servants left."

Dante approached the fallen man and the soldier attending him. "How is he?"

The soldier turned. "He will be all right, minor wound."

Dante looked around the grand home, once a source of laughter and gaiety, now a shambles. A sad, melancholy air hung over the once bright place.

He walked to the other soldier who was maneuvering furniture back into place. "Roberto said he would post a guard."

"Yes, Signor Dante, there will be a guard day and night until we are sure there is no danger. I will be here tonight."

"Good."

Dante walked into the street. The rampaging soldiers had moved on, taking any easily carried valuables with them. The noise had gone down. Dark smoke still drifted around, but except for an occasional muffled moan, the street was deathly still. The three horses were tethered nearly.

A high wooden gate stood ajar at the side of the house. He walked to it and swung it wide open. It led back and behind the building to an inner courtyard. Dante untied two of the horses and took them into the courtyard, bolting the gate behind him.

At the rear of the house was a small garden area with wrought iron table and chairs. At the far end of the property was a small, covered carriage sitting alongside a stable. He led the horses toward the stable, the odor of animals flowing out of the small building. Dante tied the two animals to a post, returned to the garden and collapsed into one of the chairs.

He had not realized how tired he was. For a moment he sat totally still, hardly breathing. Then he took a large breath and let it out slowly. The rear door of the house opened and Francesca walked quickly toward him.

"Signor Dante, you must be hungry. Let me bring you something."

"Nothing fancy, Signora, perhaps some bread, cheese and wine."

"Some fruit, also?"

"Yes, Signora. That would be fine."

He stretched his legs under the table. The smell of smoke seemed to be lessening, and it did not bother his breathing. Francesca quickly returned with a platter containing dark bread, white cheese, grapes, a pitcher of water and one of wine, two goblets.

Dante looked and smiled. "Are you joining me, Signora?"

She flushed and for the first time permitted a small chuckle. "No, Signor. I thought Signora Gentucca might come outside."

"Why don't you go and check on her and your husband?"

"Si Signor, grazie."

He broke the bread, cut some cheese, and poured a glass of wine. The sun was warm and pleasant on his face. The cheese was sharp, the wine soft and round. His eyes closed.

He blinked and sat up in his chair. She was near, across from him, smiling. The sunshine was now muted.

"How long did I doze?"

"About two hours."

"Have you eaten?

"I was waiting for you."

"I could have slept for a day. You need your strength."

"I am not worried now."

Dante smiled. "Water or wine?"

"Definitely the wine."

He reached for the wine pitcher, turned over her glass and filled it to the brim.

"You are generous with my wine, Signor Poet. Are you trying to take advantage of me?"

He leaned back and chuckled. "I should be so fortunate. You are a properly married woman."

The smile left her face, and she nodded and sipped the wine.

He looked at her as he poured some wine for himself. "Are you adequate financially?"

"Yes, my husband was careful. Matters are in good shape."

"Where are your children?"

"Elena is married, Paolo still single. When Lord Uggucione's army approached, Elena, her husband and Paolo fled. They are safe."

"I am surprised they did not take you with them."

"They tried. I refused."

Dante nodded. "You always were a brave one."

"And perhaps a bit foolish."

"Oh, I do not know. Matters worked out for you."

She smiled again. "Yes, you came just in time. I'm sorry circumstances have not been so kind to you."

Dante met her direct eyes. "Well, Providence is strange. I am in the midst of a great writing project. Perhaps if my life had been peaceful and settled, I would be a politician without time for writing."

"Dante Alighieri would always find time to write."

The sun was setting. Dante talked back and forth with her, oiling the conversation with his wit and charm. They laughed and sparred verbally. Night fell quickly.

She began to rise and he moved to pull out her chair. They walked toward the house and she hooked her arm inside his.

The rear door opened into a small kitchen area. The two servants sat at a table, eating soup. The woman quickly rose, and the man attempted to stand.

"No, Giorgio. Please, you are weak." Gentucca said, placing her hand lightly on his shoulder. He relaxed.

Dante said, "Where is the guard?"

"Outside the front."

"Has he eaten?"

"Of course, Signor Dante."

Alighieri looked at Gentucca and motioned that he was going outside. She nodded.

The soldier was on the street beside the front door, sitting in a chair. He rose as Dante approached.

Dante met his gaze. "Is everything all right?"

"Yes, Signor. All quiet now."

"How long will you stay?"

"Another will come to relieve me at midnight."

Dante looked around. The night was still, the smoke had cleared, but the smell of burnt wood hung in the damp air. The crest of Uggucione had been fixed to the entrance.

"If you need anything before midnight, just knock on the door."

"I will be fine, Signor Alighieri."

Dante turned and went inside. Gentucca was descending the stairway.

"How is your husband?"

"The same, nothing changes. Let us sit."

"I should be going. It becomes late; a guard will be here day and night. You are safe."

"Stay the night. Paolo's room is vacant."

"I think not."

"Please, I would feel better." The twinkle returned to her eyes. "Besides, Paolo's room has books, and I remember that you can read."

Dante smiled. "A passing knowledge. As you wish, Signora."

She turned toward the kitchen. "Francesca!"

The older lady scurried out. "Yes, Signora."

"Turn down the bedclothes in Paolo's room, and put some fresh water there. Signor Alighieri will spend the night."

"*Oh, Grazie Dio!* We will feel much more safe." She bowed slightly and walked away.

Hours later Dante sat at the reading desk in Paolo's bedroom. Her son had inherited Gentucca's fine intelligence and taste for good literature. Dante rose, blew out the lamp flame and turned toward the bed when the door slowly opened. Light poured in from the hallway, and she stood silhouetted in a sheer sleeping gown, the curves of her body clearly outlined under the fabric. She closed the door slowly and the only light was a small candle she held as she moved toward him. She placed the candle on the table, put out the flame and raised her hand to his cheek.

"I am properly married, my dear Dante, but I have not been *adequately* married for a long time."

They fell onto the bed together.

Alighieri slept a dreamless night. Birds singing outside the window, morning light seeping in through the shutters, he looked up at wooden beams running across the ceiling. He turned his head. She was gone; the outline of her body was on the bedclothes, and the citrus smell of her perfume lingered.

He sat up. All the nervous energy of the previous day had vanished. His body was light, his mind unusually blank and clear. He moved to the window and pushed open the wooden frame. Sunshine danced in, flowed past him over the reading table and ran up the door. He poured water into the wash basin near the window and splashed his face.

He turned back to the window; the smell of freshly baked bread rode in on the breeze. He was ravenous. Dressing quickly, he walked out on the landing and headed down the stairs toward the odor of the bread.

Francesca was alone in the kitchen, humming and cutting bread and washing some pears. *"Buon Giorno, Signor Dante. Come stai?"*

"I slept well, Francesca. Where is the lady?"

"In the garden, may I make you an egg?"

"Please."

"Bread, fruit? We have some milk still. Coffee?"

He nodded, seated himself at the table and watched her preparation.

Dante remained in Lucca for months. Matters settled down, and the life of the city resumed, but with new managers. Some nights he stayed at the fortress with his friend Uggucione; some nights he stayed with Signora Morla.

Late one afternoon they sat in her garden. Gentucca chattered on, eyes flashing, voice bright. Suddenly she paused.

"You are quiet."

"I am leaving, my dear."

"Will you always be so restless?

"God knows."

He looked at her. "I must get back to my writing."

"Write here."

"No, Lord Uggucione is a mercenary commander, not an administrator. I doubt he will be here very much longer. Della Scala is a settled man and a good ruler in Verona. I work well under those circumstances."

Her eyes misted. "I hope your stay has been pleasant."

He placed his hand upon hers. "It has been divine."

Lucca

Lucca is a city of music. Like Dante, the greatest son of Florence, the composer Giacomo Puccini was unwelcome in Lucca, his hometown during his own lifetime. And like Dante he is now revered by the city that spurned him.

Puccini was a bit of a cad in a strait-laced society. His family, particularly his father and uncle, were prominent church musicians, but Giacomo realized at an early age that his future and passion lay with opera. He pursued his music and his libertine lifestyle. Therefore he resided not in Lucca but in Torre Del Lago, on the sea nearby.

Today Puccini has been readopted by his hometown, and his spirit haunts Lucca. Music drifts through the ancient city, which is completely enclosed by massive brick ramparts. Inside the walls the ancient streets wander in a late Middle Ages pattern that would look familiar to both Puccini and Dante today.

The walls represent a movement through time. The first walls enclosing Lucca were built during the time of ancient Rome. For over a thousand years not much happened to the edges of Lucca. Then beginning in the 11th century the borders began to move. Three more sets of walls were built over the next six hundred years expanding because of defense, growing population, then defense again. The last set of walls took over one hundred years to complete and were finished around 1650. In a word they are massive.

Two and one-half miles in circumference with eleven ramparts and six huge gates that automobiles drive through today. Vast quantities of dirt were hauled in and piled on the inside of the wall creating a structure thirty meters wide at the base. Originally the gates had drawbridges that spanned a thirty-meter-wide ditch constructed on the outside and filled with water. Trees were planted on the inside mound of dirt to pack it down and provide wood for Lucca in the event of siege. All the trees outside the wall for a considerable distance were removed to deny any attacker using them.

The ramparts housed military garrisons of soldiers and there were as many as 125 huge weapons placed on the top of the walls. Long range artillery, guns firing metal cannonballs, and stone hurling cannons.

Why this tremendous defensive construction? Powerful Florence was nearby and expanding. So was military technology. Long range artillery was now the great threat. At one point the dominion of Florence extended to a town only nine miles from Lucca.

What happened? Nothing.

Lucca was never attacked and the threat faded. Today the walls serve a more beautiful purpose. A wide promenade runs along the crest of the walls. Large shade trees, water fountains, children's playground equipment, and the people of Lucca, strolling along their unique, peaceful boulevard, originally built for war.

My wife and I entered the church of San Giovanni our first evening in Lucca and took our seats on simple chairs before a grand piano backed by ceiling-high posters, photos of Puccini from various times during his life. The young playboy, the middle-aged man of culture, the contemplative older man, always with his trademark dark mustache and cigarette. That night's pianist entered to applause, then a series of vocalists came and went, each singing segments from Puccini's various operas.

All of the performers were quite good; some were exquisite. We returned night after night. On the second evening the tenor was exceptionally fine. Along with a woman soprano and a male bass he performed pieces of "Madame Butterfly."

After the finish we filed out and waited on the church steps hoping to meet the stars. They were very approachable, extremely happy that listeners cared enough to congratulate them. At some level all artists live for the appreciation of the beauty they create.

Stefano, the tenor, told us of his struggles. Night after night he traveled to different spots in Italy trying to make a living singing. I was reminded that the famous tenor, Luciano Pavarotti, was a schoolteacher in Modena desiring very much to make a living as an opera singer, but unsure he could do it. Today we find it unbelievable that anyone as great as Pavarotti could have doubts, but when you see the depth of talent in Italy you begin to understand.

In America one wonders what is the fascination with opera. To those of us unschooled in this art form, it seems simply loud, repetitive singing in an unknown language, which of course it is. But listening to these fine everyday performers in Italy, my puzzlement began to fade.

In Italy opera is in the blood. It is hard wired into Italian DNA. As with any great art, opera is best performed in its country of origin by people who understand at the most primal level what it is all about. The drama, the passion, the tragedy, the heartbreak is all part of great life, deep life, real life, and most importantly communal life. Listening to opera in a simple local church, performed by local talent for a modest fee, is the real way to experience it. You are gripped in a way that television or a grand American opera house just can't duplicate. As one performance reached its climax my wife tugged on my sleeve and pointed at her arm. Goose bumps ran up it.

Stefano and his friends said their good-byes. He was on his way to the next city. Vasso and I wandered the streets, traveling up Via Fillungo, the main walking street in the evenings. We headed toward the Piazza dell'Anfiteatro Romano.

That's right; the name is exactly what you might guess. A piazza built on the same site with the exact dimensions as the original Roman Amphitheater. Standing in the middle of the piazza today with bars and restaurants lining the oval perimeter where spectators once cheered, you can almost hear the roar of the crowds. Fortunately the blood has long since been washed away.

We strolled back toward our hotel, and as we passed an ancient palazzo, modern piano music drifted out. We walked through a covered passageway into a garden courtyard converted into a restaurant-bar where more young Italian talent was displayed for a pittance. We took an open table beside the pianist Matteo and ordered light food and a glass of wine. Jazz, rock and Italian folk tunes flowed one after another, mixed with some of the musician's own compositions. When Matteo discovered we were from the states he launched into a series of American show tunes and popular music. He played on and on, driven by his passion, never taking a break. Finally, eyes heavy we were compelled to leave and felt just as obligated to purchase one of his CDs, the only way we could think to say thanks for his kindness and the pleasant finale to a wonderful day.

The next evening we were back at the church for our nightly injection of Puccini. One man and one woman performed several arias. The man was tall with a good voice, but when the blonde opened her mouth, her voice was a resonating torrent cascading through the nave, desperately seeking an exit. After an hour our senses were pleasantly stunned and we filed out. Moving my legs seemed odd, almost difficult after giving myself totally to overpowering sound for so long. It's like one of my senses (hearing) had been so saturated and numbed that using another part of my body was awkward.

Quietly we waited on the outside steps, alone in the darkness. The soprano exited with a thin, longhaired young man. Silvia and her husband Richard lived near Florence. She would have her real debut in Milan at La Scala next year. We mentioned that last night we met and spoke with Stefano.

"Stefano!" Silvia gasped. "He's my tenor!"

"You would sing well with him, Silvia," I replied. "His voice is strong, like yours."

She nodded and smiled.

I suggested to Vasso that she invite Silvia and her husband for dinner. Soon we were heading toward the center of the walled city.

"I know a good restaurant," Silvia said.

We came to the place she had in mind, but it was closed for the night so we continued winding through the streets until we found another restaurant. She and Richard said their goodbyes and departed.

I looked at Vasso. "I thought they were going to join us."

"No. There was a misunderstanding. They must get home to their children. Grandma is watching them."

The kindness of Italians touches me. Silvia and her husband just wandered over half the center city to point out a restaurant to two strangers.

Our last morning in Lucca. Wrapped in sunshine we followed a narrow street to an obscure church, asking passersby on the way to make sure we didn't miss it. It was a small ancient chapel. A sign on the building next door proclaimed "Music School of Lucca." We entered the church and no more than a dozen audience chairs filled the tiny sanctuary. Exactly on the hour twelve musicians filed in, carrying various stringed instruments. For the next forty-five minutes the conductor led his artists in a series of separate interludes. After each piece he paused for the hearty applause. He was short, young, very dark and beaming. So pleased to be doing that thing in life he loved beyond measure. His face glowed more and more, shining with a thin film of perspiration, reaching a climax of radiance at the finale. He couldn't be happier with an audience of a thousand.

Musical Lucca.

*****

Dante spent two more years with his friend, della Scala in Verona. Matters became strained. The Poet was a man of solitude. His work was the center of his life. Increasingly, his fame spread throughout Italy. "The Inferno," destined to become the most famous part of his great trilogy was finished and copies circulated throughout the land. His fame increased. More and more often, he was called to join in the life of the court, and it didn't suit him. Frivolity was not in his nature, and he was obsessed with finishing his masterwork.

In 1318, a letter arrived. He opened it.

Dear Signor Dante Alighieri, esteemed poet,

I am Guido Novello da Polenta, Lord of Ravenna. My uncle Bernadino was your friend. He always spoke of you in the highest terms even though his friendship with you was long ago. His sister Francesca was my aunt.

We are fortunate in Ravenna to live in a lovely city with an agreeable climate. As I am sure you know, we have a glorious history for an Italian city, blessed with a unique Byzantine past.

We are at peace in our troubled world. I maintain a strong military. My object for a peaceful life is to enjoy and cultivate the arts for I believe that is our highest calling, a sacred calling. I have gathered intellectuals and literary men here to encourage and continue the culture of Ravenna as a place of learning.

I extend to you an urgent invitation to join us here. You would be under my protection, and I would provide a very adequate subsistence for you. I would ask only that you contribute to the cultural life of our commune, which you would do by your mere presence. No other conditions. Our great city would profit so much as home to the greatest poet of our age.

Please know that I would consider it a great honor to be your host, not the least reason being the memory of my fine uncle who always counted you as a friend of trust.

I have read portions of your "Inferno," and it is enthralling. Please allow me the honor of being your patron for the next portion of your great work.

With highest hopes for your positive response, respectfully,

Guido Novello da Polenta, Ravenna

Dante placed the letter aside. He had heard of this younger Guido, the grandson of the older Guido. What he had heard he liked. In some ways, young Guido resembled the sort of model monarch Dante had long envisioned to rule over the Holy Roman Empire. A man of strength who used the peace to promote arts and learning. Guido would never have great powers over a large area, but Ravenna had a glorious history. Dante immediately rose and walked toward the rooms of his patron, Della Scala, to tell him he was departing for Ravenna.

The Poet's meeting with Guido in Ravenna was everything he had hoped for. The young ruler was intelligent, cultured and a bit of a poet himself. They formed a quick and fast friendship, and the younger man was a bit in awe of the man he referred to as *"Sommo Poeta,"* Greatest Poet. In this Guido was not just flattering, he was truly prophetic.

Da Polenta immediately offered to also support Dante's grown children, and soon Jacob, Pietro and Antonia joined their father in Ravenna. The court was truly a place of culture and learning. Dante was quickly surrounded by literary friends and admirers, including the Florentine exiles Pietro Giardini, Dino Perini, and Fiduccio de Milotti. He loved talking with them in the Tuscan dialect. He began his lively and humorous correspondence with Giovanni del Virgilio, the Bolognese poet. No doubt since Dante's Comedy was so influenced by Virgil's "Aeneid," Giovanni of Virgil, an avid student of the old master was a great help and encouragement to Alighieri.

The fine churches of Ravenna were a joy to the aging poet who had finally set politics completely aside. Dante gave lectures around the city on a vast variety of subjects. He even traveled back to Verona to give scientific lectures there. Del Virgilio suggested a prestigious literary award for Alighieri, but Dante declined to travel to Bologna to accept until his Comedy was entirely complete. And finish it he did. Soon copies of the complete masterwork began to circulate around the country.

Antonia took her vows to become a nun, entered a convent, and took the name Sister Beatrice, a telling tribute to Dante's muse. The brilliant, fierce, temperamental genius Dante Alighieri had finally found some degree of peace.

Ravenna

Ravenna is the Italian town that time has forgotten. Thousands of years ago it began to grow Venice-like on several islands in the mouth of the Po River where it enters the Adriatic Sea. Eventually Ravenna developed into a strategic seaport during the early phases of the Roman Empire.

Rome and Italy weakened until in the fifth century A.D. Ravenna like Rome, fell to Germanic tribes from the north. However, in the middle of the sixth century the Byzantine emperor Justinian "retook" the city. During the years that followed artisans, builders, bureaucrats and scholars flooded in from the Byzantine east, and Ravenna swelled in prominence and size. As time went by the port silted up and the sea retreated, leaving the central city inland. Today the harbor is over four miles from the ancient center of town, and the surrounding territory is no longer marsh, but fertile farmland.

We arrived on a midsummer afternoon after driving several hours in heavy rain. A girl at the tourist information office directed us to our hotel, several blocks north of the town center. It was the Hotel Diana.

The next morning after breakfast I descended the stairway to the lobby and found Vasso talking with a man at the reception desk. He gripped the frame of a massive painting resting on the floor, leaning against him. It was a picture of a woman painted in ancient style. She held a bow and arrow and at her feet lay a large deer, obviously a victim of her marksmanship.

Phillip was the owner of the hotel. In his forties, well built and full of youthful energy, he talked about his experiences as a college football player in the United States. Phillip couldn't do enough for us. He gave us copies of a local book about Ravenna. When we told him we would visit Lake Maggiore next he said,

"I have a cousin who rents speedboats there. I will call her and reserve one for you. For free. No charge."

When I hesitated, he replied with a confidence part athletic and part pure Italian.

"Don't worry. It is very easy!"

My wife and I finally pulled ourselves away from his generosity, and as we walked toward town I asked, "What was Phillip doing with that large painting?"

"Oh. After I met him, I said, 'Hotel Diana? How did you come up with that name? I see no Diana around here.' He immediately went downstairs to his office and dragged that painting up to the lobby. That was Diana, goddess of the hunt."

One thing about modern Ravenna is astonishing, and that alone makes the city a five star attraction. It has the finest Byzantine mosaics in the world, leaving notable cities like Venice and Constantinople/Istanbul far behind. Vasso and I entered the dark, brooding, brown brick church of San Vitale. The rubble of centuries had piled up around the large building so the main floor of the church was half underground. We descended a gloomy staircase and walked through the entrance … cool, dark, tomb-like. As we passed around a wall I stopped, stunned. It was as if a huge spotlight had suddenly been flicked on, the massive domed interior flooded me with light and life. A dazzling sanctuary of bright green, blue and gold mosaic walls and ceiling surrounded and left me in a state of awe. It had been a long time since I felt such a spirit of reverence. The mosaics depicted the Byzantine rulers of the city and various stories from the Bible. Sitting there for over an hour I reviewed the great religious myths of Christian culture glowing on the walls. Never have green and blue mixed together so well. Time stood still.

After a while, time seemed to begin again, as it always does. We left the green/blue cocoon and leaving the church grounds came to the tomb of Galla Placida. A small chapel-like structure in the form of a cross, you enter and once more are rewarded with wonderful mosaics. The interior is quite dark, and the ceiling sparkles with tiny light reflections like brilliant stars on a cloudless night in the deep countryside. It is said the great American composer, Cole Porter, took inspiration from this interior on his honeymoon in the 1920s and then composed his lovely ballad, "Night and Day."

Finally, silently Vasso and I departed and walked toward the Piazza del Popolo, the central square of the old city. Gradually I became aware of gentle voices around us. I looked up and the Byzantine faces from the mosaics of the church had fallen onto the shoulders of the local people walking around us. Olive-skinned, heart-shaped faces with high cheekbones and severely tapering chins. Large, dark, almond-shaped eyes with prominent pointed noses. There was a distinct variation in appearance and manners between these people in Ravenna and natives in other parts of Italy. It was like a bunch of Greeks had been dropped into this Italian city. Strolling down sun-drenched cobblestone streets I looked into the grand, quiet courtyards of ancient palaces, fountains softly splashing in their centers, and a Middle Eastern atmosphere drifted out to me. Christian, yes. Western, no. The spirit and look of ancient Byzantium have been preserved in this most unusual of places. Travel through time.

Over the next several days we spent time wandering through the streets of the center city. We searched for the best café. One afternoon we noticed two uniformed *carabinieri* (policemen) in their wonderful uniforms: starched white shirts with nicely creased black pants, crimson stripes running down the outside length of each trouser leg. We watched them enter

Theodora's Café on an ancient arcaded street that whispers with the ghosts of Constantinople. They enjoyed a drink and the generous appetizers so we imitated their example, and Theodora's became our daily watering spot.

We explored the church of San Apollinare Nuovo, its long nave bordered on each side by a series of Corinthian columns, each topped by a Christian cross. Above each row of columns was a long, brilliant golden mosaic of saintly figures, which preserved the segregated decorum of Greek churches, a line of female saints were on the left wall, a line of martyred men on the right.

As I bought an English newspaper at a kiosk near one of the piazzas, Vasso disappeared into a nearby dress shop. After scanning the news stories for a few minutes, I followed into the boutique and found her near the counter talking with two women. Antonella was the store manager. Tall, slim and blonde, she must have been in her late thirties. She wore a form-fitting black dress that made it hard for any man to look away. Her companion was shorter, dark-haired, and the three women laughed and joked like old friends. I looked into the classic Byzantine faces chatting with my Greek wife, and I realized, more than old friends, these three could be sisters through time.

After a few minutes a gentleman entered. He had thick salt and pepper hair, squinty eyes and glasses. He chatted quite comfortably with Antonella. It was obvious they knew each other well, and he didn't come into the shop looking for a dress.

After a few minutes, Antonella introduced the gentleman. "This is my friend, Carlo."

"I thought he was your husband." I replied.

Carlo glanced briefly at the floor and said, "I wish Antonella would marry me."

She looked at us with a broad, relaxed smile and said nothing. The natural confidence of a liberated, desired woman who has the choice and initiative in her own hands.

Carlo departed, and the three ladies began complimenting each other on how good they looked for their ages. They began with my wife who was the oldest of the three, but Vasso's actual age remained classified information.

They wanted me to join their little bit of drama, and any man would be a fool to resist the multiplied charms of three attractive women.

"How old are you, Antonella?" I asked.

"Guess."

As if I was at an auction, I offered a low bid. "Thirty-five."

"I'm forty-three." She smiled.

I looked at the floor and muttered, "You're lying."

The smile broadened.

Her companion looked at me. "How old am I?"

"Twenty-four." I said quickly.

"I'm twenty-nine."

"You're lying, too."

More laughter. It was time for Vasso and me to leave. The fun was peaking.

*****

In 1321 a ship of Ravenna and a Venetian ship collided in the Adriatic, resulting in a skirmish between the crews. Venice was a great sea power, and the doge of Venice, Giovanni Soranzo, was a powerful and fierce man who maintained his kingdom and reputation at all costs.

Dante sat at his writing desk in his small home near da Polenta's palace. In Ravenna. A sharp knock came from the door. He rose and opened the door and was shocked to see Lord Guido, two seated horsemen behind him.

"Young Lord, please come in. What brings you here?"

"Great Poet, I have a favor to ask."

Dante smiled and beckoned toward a table and chairs. "A favor? Excellency, you have made these past few years the happiest of my life, and you have asked for nothing in return. Whatever you wish, if it is in my power, I am happy to oblige."

Guido quickly detailed the events of the altercation. "Venice is powerful. We are small. I must play my strongest card. You, in addition to many other things, are a gifted diplomat. Would you go to Venice to negotiate a peace settlement?"

Dante looked at his host for a moment. "Happily I will go, but I have not gone on a diplomatic mission for some years." His eyes twinkled. "Perhaps I am out of form."

Guido laughed out loud. "Out of form! I would rather have you out of practice than Cicero in the prime of life."

Dante reached over and patted his friend on the arm. Switching to the familiar tongue he said, "Guido, would you like something to drink?"

The young man nodded.

Dante rose, retreated to the kitchen and returned with two goblets and a bottle of white wine. He sat and poured two portions, the men clinked glasses and relaxed. After some time, Dante said, "Guido, what is on your mind?"

"Dante, you are not only a very able diplomat, your prestige has grown and grown. Your fame can help offset Ravenna's smaller size in regard to Venice."

"That is good thinking," said Dante. "When would you like me to go?"

"We should send someone within a week. Can you be ready?"

"Of course."

Guido embraced the older man. "Thank you, good friend."

"The least I can do for all your kindness."

They walked to the door. Guido turned. "I will have all the preparations made. You will go by sea in seven days. I will keep you informed."

"As you wish."

He was gone.

Within a week, Dante was aboard a merchant vessel, sailing north to Venice. Several other members of Guido Novello's inner circle of advisors traveled with him. Dante was designated as "chief diplomat." He stood at the rail with the captain in late afternoon sunshine as the islands of the Serene Republic came into view. They floated like great ships in the lagoon. Church bell towers and the towers of palaces pointed upward like the masts of war galleys.

The ship slid into the main docking place, sail coming down, as ropes shot out like cannon fire to eager hands on the pier. The boat was quickly secured.

Four men in government robes emblazoned with the crest of Venice waited on the dock. Dante thanked the captain, then the Poet and his group of emissaries stepped onto the wooden dock.

One of the Venetians stepped forward. "Signor Alighieri?"

Dante moved to greet him. "I am Dante Alighieri."

"I am Gandolfo Orsini, first secretary to His Excellency, Doge Soranzo. Welcome to the Most Serene Republic of Venice. Please follow me."

Dante smiled inwardly and thought, *"We are not here because of serene behavior."*

The group from Ravenna followed the Venetians away from the harbor. They came to St. Mark's square, passed the magnificent basilica and came to the Doge's Palace.

Orsini said, "Signor Alighieri, there are quarters for you and your emissaries in rooms adjoining the palace. Our servants will direct you there and see that you are settled. His Excellency extends an invitation to you personally, Signor Alighieri, to dine with him this evening in his private home quarters."

"That would be fine."

"Very well. Someone will call for you after sunset."

Dante and his colleagues settled in their rooms. He took a short nap, awoke, dressed appropriately for dinner, waited for his escort and thought about the situation. His knowledge of the doge and the situation was meager.

The underlying cause of the incident between the Venetians and the Ravenesi was rivalry over the lucrative black market salt trade. The current doge, Soranzo, was a very able man. A former military general and admiral, he had risen through the ranks and made his reputation as a successful commander in sea battles in the Greek Aegean Sea. The Venetians, the Genovese and the Byzantines all struggled for control of the Aegean. Soranzo had victories against the Byzantines that moved him up the political power ladder.

The Doge was basically the chief government official of Venice. The office was supposedly for life, but some doges had been removed forcibly from office. Most often though, upon the death of a doge, his successor was elected by consensus of the other political leaders.

Soranzo was ready to assume power in 1310, but an ugly incident delayed his appointment. His son-in-law and that young man's father had tried to help overthrow the government authority. They failed. The father, Soranzo's son-in-law and his wife, Soranzo's daughter, had been banished from the city. Rumor had it that they were living in hiding somewhere in the Aegean islands.

Soranzo was not implicated in the conspiracy. However, the nasty business delayed his ascension to doge by two years. He had now held the office for nine years, and there was every indication he was strong enough to continue.

After the recent naval incident, Soranzo had moved quickly. He allied with the city of Forli to oppose Ravenna, and he had secured the neutrality of Rimini, Cesena, Imola and Faenza. Guido Novello was effectively surrounded geographically and quite nervous. Obviously, Venice had the much stronger hand. Hence, Dante's mission.

As the light of the day died, a knock came on the door. Dante opened it to find a palace servant.

"Signor Alighieri?"

"Yes."

"His Excellency requests that I escort you to the banquet room."

"I am ready."

The servant led Dante through winding corridors that eventually opened into a large banquet hall. Perhaps a dozen men were clustered around a dining table, silver candlesticks casting light along the plates and dinner settings. After the normal pleasantries and introductions, the guests seated themselves.

With the exception of the Doge and his assistants, the other guests were envoys from the city-states that Venice had enlisted as allies in the dispute. Dante was seated at an inferior position at the foot of the table. The Doge sat at head of the table, far from the Poet.

The various courses arrived, and the conversations began to buzz. No one spoke to Dante, and he did not try to initiate any small talk.

Finally, the main fish course arrived. All the envoys and the Doge received ample portions. Dante's fish was significantly smaller than that of the other guests.

Alighieri's lips tightened slightly. He reached to his plate, grasped the fish and lifted it to his ear as if listening for it to speak to him.

At the head of the table, the Doge watched this, and the edge of his mouth turned up slightly. "Signor Alighieri, what is this unusual behavior?"

Dante said, "As I knew the father of this fish met his death in these waters, I asked this little fellow of news of his father."

"And what did he answer?"

"He told me he was too small to remember much about his father, but that I would surely be able to learn what I wanted from the older fish, who could give me the news I desired."

The Doge smiled and beckoned for one of the waiters, then whispered to the servant who hurried away. Soon he returned with a large fish portion and placed it before Dante. The rest of the evening passed without incident.

The mission was difficult for Dante. The Doge was unyielding. When Dante spoke in Latin, he was asked to speak in Italian. When he spoke in classical Italian, his hosts replied in their Venetian dialect, acting as if they did not understand him. Sometimes they simply did not reply. Dante's only success was arranging a return visit in September to continue negotiations.

Venice

During the four wonderful years I was in Italy, my family and I lived about one hour north of Venice. Everything that can possibly be said of this city has already been said countless times through the centuries, but here goes.

I always traveled to Venice by train. In a city where the streets are waterways, coming by car just seemed a little strange. My strongest memories of this magical town are damp water buses, stagnant canals, mildewed buildings and the glorious light. All over Italy the sunlight is magical, but in Venice the brilliant, cold light of winter is a clean, luminescent vapor. It flows through narrow passageways and seeps around corners as you move through the mist like a fish in a strangely lit aquarium. You feel it drifting past you; it is part light, part fog, part chill dampness.

St. Mark's Square is the heart of Venice with Florian's Café, Harry's Bar and of course, St. Mark's Basilica. The church doesn't seem quite sure whether it is a western cathedral or an eastern sanctuary. It is a glorious hodgepodge of mosaics, statues and jewels. Four huge bronze horses from Constantinople stand guard on the upper facade of the basilica. Entering through the front doors you stand in a huge golden igloo, sparkling mosaic pieces covering the domed interior high above you. The remains of Mark, the poverty-stricken evangelist ironically lie in a priceless, jewel encrusted coffin on the altar.

Venice is seldom comfortable. When it is, it is priceless. I most preferred wintertime. Even though I hate the cold, it was worth it to experience Venice in that way. And at one of the colder moments of the year, the grand spectacle of *Carnevale* takes place.

In the two weeks before Lent the streets and squares of Venice fill with the most creative costumes imaginable. Half-face masks expertly constructed of light brown feathers hide the eyes and noses of fashionable matrons. Huge flat hats with miniature replicas of St. Mark's square and its buildings adorn the heads of young men. All kinds of outlandish and extensive outfits joyfully compete for your attention.

But always there are the beautiful costumed women. My favorites were the young girls dressed in nuns' habits. Long black robes and starched black and white hoods hid all flesh except tiny cute faces. Suddenly one of the pretend nuns sat on a stone bench and crossed her legs, and a long slit opened from ankle to upper thigh, revealing a shapely feminine leg in a shocking, black fishnet stocking. She saw my surprise and flashed a smile that was dazzling.

My wife and I departed late one afternoon, pleasantly satisfied after this visual feast of disguises. Walking ahead of us was a young couple, each wrapped from head to toe as bandaged mummies. The girl and her companion were perhaps ten years younger than us, and she repeatedly glanced back to catch my eye, giving me one of those magnetic smiles. She was so happy to be part of this masquerade.

This is another reason foreign men find Italian women so alluring. They love to engage your attention with their beauty. It is not so much flirting as it is their own personal enjoyment of your appreciation of their attractiveness. And of course they know! All women know that, it's just that Italian women unabashedly delight in it. On the other hand, maybe it is flirting. Italian style.

The entire four years I lived in Italy I had only one bad restaurant meal outside of Venice. I remember every detail because it was so unusual. The town, the waiter, the weather at my outside table. This is one of the remarkable things about Italy. It is so difficult to get poor food. Except in Venice.

I had the hardest time finding a good, affordable restaurant. Good, yes. Affordable, no. I finally gave up and often ate in the train station, which was really a lot better than it sounds. Maybe it was simply because Venice is such a tourist trap. Maybe I just didn't know where to go. But in other towns and cities, I didn't have to know. I just went.

Once you go beyond the common tourist haunts like St. Mark's Square, Venice in summer can be hauntingly beautiful, but you must get away from the crowds. The city has the deep melancholy feeling of a New England town in autumn. The dark green shutters of beige apartment buildings are closed up tight. The tiny piazzas are empty of human movement and flooded with liquid sunshine. The only sounds are small fountains softly splashing. Even the birds are careful to flutter quietly.

Venice is constantly dying. The centuries of the Serene Republic are long gone. Every year fewer and fewer natives can afford to live in the city. The buildings slowly sink in the submerged mud. The sea slowly rises. In the wintertime, the locals spend most of their time in rubber boots, wading through *alta acqua*, high water.

Venice has been dying for a long time, and it will continue dying for a long time. But one thing is certain. This grand old lady, floating with severe, erotic dignity on the calm sea, reflecting her glorious past in pristine, misty light … she will outlive us all.

*****

Circumstances required Dante to travel overland back to Ravenna from Venice. In the hot humid summer of 1321, fifty-five year old Dante Alighieri traveled through the marshland that lies between Venice and Ravenna. He contracted a fever and arriving in his adopted city, the Summo Poeta died several weeks later of malaria. Guido Novello ensured he was buried with great dignity. An elaborate funeral procession made its way to the burial site. The coffin was open, and a copy of the Divine Comedy laid on the chest of the body.

Ravenna has moved to its own beat over the centuries, its eternally personal cadence. A prominent place in the center of Italy's Adriatic coast, yet a place that is not entirely Italian. Little wonder it welcomed the wandering exile so out of step with his powerful hometown. Yet here he fit in. A place with a kindred spirit. Like Dante, Ravenna is intellectual, independent and deeply religious. A place apart, and determined enough to stay that way. Besides the echoes of Byzantium, the other spirit of Ravenna is the spirit of Dante. There is a Via Beatrice Alighieri, a Via Pietro Alighieri and a Via Dante Alighieri. At the end of Via Dante is a simple tomb where the poet's body rests.

After a time Florence repented of its treatment of Italy's greatest writer and asked that the body be returned to its home city. But Dante had wandered enough. Ravenna simply said, "No."

The requests continued until in 1519 the Florentine Medici Pope Leo X ordered removal of the remains from Ravenna to Florence. Defying the pope, monks from a nearby cloister removed the poet's body and hid it. During World War II the bones were again hidden, and again returned to the original grave. So even in death the Poet's body has continued to wander to some degree, but in the end Dante remains in his adopted city.

That is Ravenna. The Italian city where the spirit of ancient Byzantium mingles with the spirit of Dante.

Ravenna is a time machine.

The Church Moves On

After the death of Dante the Church looked more and more for support from French kings. With European political pressures and wars, bribery and corruption in the church, and the stresses of Roman politics the situation grew chaotic. The last half of the 13th century had witnessed a rapid succession of at least thirteen popes. From time to time a pontiff was forced to flee Rome until finally the papal throne was moved to Avignon in France. The papacy remained there for seventy years.

Finances and efficient administration were strengthening within the church. Popes organized and equipped armies. In 1377, the papacy left Avignon to return to Rome. An amazing age, born in the minds and lives of Frederick and Dante, dawned on the western world.

The Renaissance was a remarkable period, and certainly the church reflected that. A brilliant rediscovery of the beauty of classical learning spawned creativity in the arts, notably in books and buildings. Rome was rebuilt in a grand style and so was the church. The secular dream was taking root, and for now the church was a partner.

The Vatican Library was established, papal armies swept invaders from the peninsula and the bishops of Rome displayed their mistresses within the Vatican. The church commissioned masterpieces of painting and sculpture. Like many family-minded Italians the popes took good care of their relatives. Nephews, brothers and cousins received lucrative positions. Non-family members bought the office of cardinal.

All this building and battling took a great deal of money and corruption was everywhere. Ethical men within Italy and without called for reform. Finally an obscure German theology professor, trained as a monk, harnessed a profound religious experience and the power of a new technology to change the course of history. His name was Martin Luther.

Luther went through a spiritual crisis and transformation. He desperately sought satisfaction, and he couldn't find it within church theology and practice. It didn't help that the Roman church was hawking spiritual blessing for money in the crassest terms. Luther found his peace with God in the phrase, "the just shall live by faith." Armed with his newfound zeal, he condemned the teaching and corruption of the church and he found a ready audience.

The newly invented printing press propelled Luther's ideas and teaching to peasants who longed for spiritual liberation. At the upper end of the economic spectrum the wealthy and powerful saw Luther's message as justification to capture church buildings and property for the state. In Rome the popes didn't grasp the significance of what was happening. The Protestant Reformation swept across Europe.

Secure in their form of Christianity the popes had drifted into politics, war and money. Now a rival spiritual movement threatened their influence. The kings of Europe felt their power surge and the Catholic Church weaken.

In the year 1527 the strongest ruler in Europe was Charles V of Spain who also held power in Austria and Germany. His army advanced on Rome and devastated it. The pope fled.

Peace was secured and the pope returned, but Rome was shattered. The Renaissance faded away; the Catholic Counter-Reformation began. The most visible outward sign was the rebuilding of Rome. Nearing the end of his life, the great Michelangelo was put in charge of making the new Saint Peter's the greatest church in Christendom.

In the years that followed there were both mediocre popes and great popes, but reform marched on. The ability of the church to compete with European rulers waned, but the authority of the pope within the Catholic Church grew and grew. In 1540 a new order with missionary zeal was authorized, the Jesuits. Losing strength in Europe, like ancient Romans the popes expanded into new frontiers, in this case ... the Americas.

Instead of direct competition with kings the church moved to influence European rulers. These monarchs were involved in a savage, dirty business ... war. The popes subsidized the armies.

But as the world moved into the 1700s, it was more often the European kings who squeezed the Church. Individual Catholic churches outside Italy came under the power of the rulers of their respective countries. The church in Rome came under siege.

In 1789 the French revolution broke out, church property was confiscated by the new government and the French clergy persecuted. On the heels of the revolution Napoleon Bonaparte descended on Italy. In February 1798 a French army entered Rome, arrested the pope and transported him to France where he died.

For the next seventeen years a crazy, seesaw power struggle waged between this French general and the popes. When Napoleon went to exile in 1815, the pope returned to Rome and the Papal States were restored. But the tide of history was changing, and incessant pressure built for the establishment of a unified Italy.

Through the early and mid-1800s, the Church was the greatest obstacle blocking unification of the country. Maybe it always had been. In the summer of 1870 the king of northern Italy, Victor Emmanuel invaded the Papal States and Rome. The pope and the Church retreated to the Vatican where they have remained ever since. Italy had finally become a united, secular country.

The Catholic Church is the most remarkable, enduring organization in the history of this planet. For better or worse, it carried Italian culture along on its miraculous journey through time. For nearly two thousand years the Italian popes were successors to the ancient emperors of Rome. Brilliant and diverse, they walked the tightrope of survival, balancing spiritual responsibility and temporal politics. Aggressive, evangelical conquerors.

They were Italians; they are survivors.

There is No Conclusion to Italy

The wonderful movie, *Cinema Paradiso,* won the Academy Award in 1989 for Best Foreign film. The musical score by Ennio Morricone is sublime. The same theme is repeated in countless variations throughout the movie, but it never grows old. Nor does the movie. In the extended, uncut version, a famous, middle-aged Italian film-maker returns to the poor, dusty Sicilian town where he grew up. He comes back for the funeral of his oldest and best friend, the projectionist at the local cinema.

There he rediscovers the love of his life. As teenagers they were tragically separated, neither knowing where the other had gone. Elena's parents took her to Tuscany; Salvatore went to Rome to work in the film industry.

As the story unfolds and Salvatore realizes what happened and the part his old friend played in the separation, he says, "Damn him!"

Elena replies, "No, if we had stayed you never would have made your movies, and that would be a shame. They are wonderful. I've seen every one.

"Don't hate him. Somehow he knew that you had another life ahead."

It has all the elements of classic Italian tragedy. Star-crossed lovers, separated forever because of destiny. Romeo and Juliet. Dante and Beatrice. Dante and his city. Frederick II and his dream. Great tragedy encompasses great life. And God or fate always holds the final hand. The only thing that is stronger than destiny is love. Destiny can separate lovers, but destiny can never destroy love.

We're born, we live and we die. But our world goes on, and somehow there is a continuum through time. Best seen perhaps in a history and culture like Italy. Here life is supreme, real and ever present. Here human beings are always paramount. Governments come and go, people survive the best they can, and in the midst of it all there is a vivid, pulsating reality in the everyday of life. If there is one thing I've learned from Italy, it's that every moment of our lives is magic. We have only to see it.

In Italy it is easy to see.

About the Author

Dr. David Lundberg holds degrees from the United States Air Force Academy, Boston University and the University of North Carolina. David is a retired, decorated Air Force officer and a retired university professor. He and his wife, Vasso now spend their winters in North Carolina and their summers in Ireland.

Made in the USA
Monee, IL
11 October 2021